Tourism Research in Ibero-America

T0300229

This comprehensive volume includes new contributions in research by Ibero-American specialists in tourism analysis. The chapters deal with outstanding areas of interest at the level of tourism research, both from the professional and academic perspectives in the Ibero-American region. The content spreads along a number of varied topics like the urban destination planning from an architectural point of view, the creation of new magic villages in Mexico, the management of natural and wildlife areas, and a new focus on the blue growth strategy from a circular economy´s perspective. There are chapters that provide new insights on cruise passengers profiling and discuss new methodologies to compute the impact of this type of vacational travelling for the territories involved. The book also examines the new areas of tourism in the market, like wine tourism and border medical tourism in Mexico.

Tourism Research in Ibero-America: Urban Destinations, Sustainable Approaches and New Products postulates new perspectives in the study of the Trans-Atlantic's shared interest for the tourism and hospitality activities, with fresh and up-to-date methodologies. It analyses the current situation of the tourism sector for the whole Ibero-American world, including The Americas, Spain, and Portugal and will be of great interest to a wide audience.

The chapters in this book were originally published as a special issue of *Anatolia*.

Andrés Artal-Tur is Associate Professor at Technical University of Cartagena (Spain). His main research interest is in tourists' behaviour, marketing, and destination planning. More recently, his focus includes the study of the host-guest relationship in tourism, the socio-cultural dimension in the sustainability of destinations, and the social implications of COVID-19 in tourists' behaviour.

Antónia Correia is Professor of Tourism Economics, University of Algarve and at the Tourism and Hospitality School at Universidade Europeia, both in Portugal. Research areas include consumer behaviour, tourism economics, and modelling. She has published more than one hundred papers in tourism, leisure, and economics journals. She is a member of the editorial boards of several leading journals including *Journal of Travel Research*, *Journal of Business Research*, *Tourism Analysis*, and *Anatolia*.

María Pilar Jiménez-Medina is Assistant Professor at Technical University of Cartagena (Spain). Her main research interest is in residents' and tourists' behaviour, marketing, and products/destinations planning. Currently, her focus includes the study of the host-guest relationship in tourism, the socio-cultural dimension in the sustainability of destinations, and the social implications of COVID-19 in residents' and tourists' behaviour.

Tourism Research in Ibero-America

Urban Destinations, Sustainable Approaches and New Products

Edited by
Andrés Artal-Tur, Antónia Correia and María Pilar Jiménez-Medina

LONDON AND NEW YORK

First published 2021
by Routledge
2 Park Square, Milton Park, Abingdon, Oxon OX14 4RN

and by Routledge
605 Third Avenue, New York, NY 10158

Routledge is an imprint of the Taylor & Francis Group, an informa business

© 2021 Taylor & Francis

British Library Cataloguing in Publication Data
A catalogue record for this book is available from the British Library

ISBN: 978-0-367-69184-4 (hbk)
ISBN: 978-0-367-69188-2 (pbk)
ISBN: 978-1-003-14078-8 (ebk)

Typeset in Minion Pro
by Newgen Publishing UK

Publisher's Note
The publisher accepts responsibility for any inconsistencies that may have arisen during the conversion of this book from journal articles to book chapters, namely the inclusion of journal terminology.

Disclaimer
Every effort has been made to contact copyright holders for their permission to reprint material in this book. The publishers would be grateful to hear from any copyright holder who is not here acknowledged and will undertake to rectify any errors or omissions in future editions of this book.

Contents

Citation Information

The following chapters were originally published in *Anatolia*, volume 30, issue 2 (June 2019). When citing this material, please use the original page numbering for each article, as follows:

For any permission-related enquiries please visit:
www.tandfonline.com/page/help/permissions

Notes on Contributors

Tindara Abbate, Department of Economics, University of Messina, Messina, Italy.

Pedro Anunciação, Department of Information Systems, (IPC), Setúbal, Portugal.

Andrés Artal-Tur, Department of Economics, Universidad Politécnica de Cartagena, Cartagena, Spain.

María Belén Cobacho-Tornel, Quantitative Methods and Computing Department, Universidad Politécnica de Cartagena, Cartagena, Spain.

Juan Andrés Bernal Conesa, CUD Centre, Technical University of Cartagena (UPCT), Santiago de la Ribera, Spain.

Antonio Juan Briones Peñalver, Department of Business Economics, Technical University of Cartagena (UPCT), Cartagena, Spain.

Antónia Correia, Faculdade de Turismo e Hospitalidade, Universidade Europeia, Lisboa, Portugal; Faculdade de Economia, Universidade do Algarve and CEFAGE, Faro, Portugal.

Giacomo Del Chiappa, Department of Business and Economics, University of Sassari, Sardinia, Italy; Senior Research Fellow, School of Tourism & Hospitality, University of Johannesburg, Johannesburg, South Africa.

María Angélica Esparza Santillana, Nursing Department, FEMAP Hospital and Hospital Ángeles of Ciudad Juárez, Ciudad Juárez, Mexico.

Alicia M. García-Amaya, Department of Urbanism, Universitat Politècnica de Valencia (UPV), Valencia, Spain.

Antonio García-Sánchez, Department of Economics, Technical University of Cartagena, Cartagena, Spain.

Jaume Guía Julve, Department of Organization, Business Management, and Product Design, University of Girona, Girona, Spain.

Maria Teresa Martínez Almanza, Social Sciences Department, Universidad Autónoma de Ciudad Juárez, Ciudad Juárez, Mexico.

Beatriz Mayén Cañavate, Department of Business Economics, Technical University of Cartagena (UPCT), Cartagena, Spain.

Javier Mendoza-Monpeán, Faculty of Business Studies, Technical University of Cartagena, Cartagena, Spain.

Santos Alonso Morales Muñoz, Social Sciences Department, Universidad Autónoma de Ciudad Juárez, Ciudad Juárez, Mexico.

José Miguel Navarro-Azorín, Department of Economics, Technical University of Cartagena, Cartagena, Spain.

Gerardo Novo, Faculty of Tourism and Gastronomy, Autonomous University of the State of Mexico, Toluca, Mexico.

Maribel Osorio, Faculty of Tourism and Gastronomy, Autonomous University of the State of Mexico, Toluca, Mexico.

María Pilar Jiménez-Medina, Department of Business Management, Technical University of Cartagena (UPCT), Cartagena, Spain.

María Pilar Peñarrubia-Zaragoza, Department of Geography, Universidad de Valencia (UV), Valencia, Spain.

Juan Ignacio Pulido-Fernández, Department of Economics, Faculty of Social and Legal Sciences, University of Jaén, Jaén, Spain.

José María Ramos-Parreño, Department of Economics, Technical University of Cartagena, Cartagena, Spain.

Marcello Risitano, Department of Management and Quantitative Studies, University of Naples Parthenope, Naples, Italy.

Ismael Manuel Rodríguez Herrera, Department of Tourism, Center of Economic and Administrative Sciences, Autonomous University of Aguascalientes, Aguascalientes, Mexico.

Leticia del Socorro Shaadi Rodríguez, Department of Tourism, Center of Economic and Administrative Sciences, Autonomous University of Aguascalientes, Aguascalientes, Mexico.

Rosa María Angélica Shaadi Rodríguez, Department of Tourism, Center of Economic and Administrative Sciences, Autonomous University of Aguascalientes, Aguascalientes, Mexico.

David Siles, Department of Economics, Technical University of Cartagena, Cartagena, Spain.

Moisés R. Simancas-Cruz, Department of Geography and History, Universidad de La Laguna (ULL), San Cristóbal de La Laguna, Spain.

Annarita Sorrentino, Department of Management and Quantitative Studies, University of Naples Parthenope, Naples, Italy.

Sergio Sotomayor, Enology Department, Autonomous University of the State of Mexico, Tenancingo, Mexico.

Rafael R. Temes-Cordovez, Department of Urbanism, Universitat Politècnica de Valencia (UPV), Valencia, Spain.

Miguel Ángel Tobarra-González, Faculty of Business Studies, Technical University of Cartagena, Cartagena, Spain.

María de Mar Vázquez-Méndez, Department of Economics, Technical University of Cartagena, Cartagena, Spain.

Preface

In line with the appealing initiative of Taylor & Francis regarding the publishing of Special Issues as Books, Routledge editors have proposed us to edit the former Special Issue in *Anatolia* journal with the new title of *Tourism Research in Ibero-America: Urban Destinations, Sustainable Approaches and New Products*, under the editorial guidance of Profs. Andrés Artal-Tur, Antónia Correia, and María Pilar Jiménez-Medina from Technical University of Cartagena, Spain (Andrés and María Pilar), and University of Algarve + Universidade Europeia de Lisboa, Portugal (Antónia).

It is for us a pleasure to revisit the papers in our former Special Issues, now giving this volume an easy-to-read format for both novel and technical readers. The current volume includes new contributions in research by Ibero-American specialists in tourism analysis. The content spreads along a number of varied topics such as the urban destination planning from an architectural point of view, the creation of new magic villages in Mexico to be visited, the management of natural and wildlife areas, and a new focus on the blue growth strategy from a circular economy's perspective. Other chapters provide new insights on the analysis of cruise passengers profiling, or about new methodologies to compute the impact of this type of vacational travelling for the territories involved. New products in the market, such as wine tourism and border medical tourism in Mexico, are also reviewed along this book. The volume provides in general new perspectives in the study of the Trans-Atlantic shared interest for the tourism and hospitality activities, with fresh and up-to-date methodologies. It is written in a non-technical style, and directed to a wide audience, including interested students, specialists, professionals, and the general public that wants to improve their knowledge on the latest advances taking place in the global tourism industry of today. We all three editors hope you enjoy the reading of this volume, making it an interesting reading for your students, interested colleagues, and all those pursuing tourism businesses at these troubling times.

Andrés Artal-Tur, Antónia Correia and María Pilar Jiménez-Medina
Cartagena, Spain & Faro, Algarve, Portugal
October 2020

Introduction

New contributions in Tourism Research in the Ibero-American world

Andrés Artal-Tur (iD) and Antónia Correia (iD)

Tourism is a fast growing industry, reaching 1.2 billion international travellers last year 2017, and with forecasted numbers of 1.8 billion in 2030 according to the World Tourism Organization. Latin countries in Europe and America are important destinations in the world tourism market. Spain received more than 82 international arrivals in 2017, ranked in second place in terms of arrivals and receipts in the UNWTO annual statistics. Portugal reached the distinction of Best Tourism Destination in the World in 2017 given by the World Travel Awards, recognizing the huge competitiveness and efforts that this country is making in the last years in order to continue growing as a global destination and for specific segments like rural or golf tourism for example. Latin America, with a variety of destinations and tourism specialization patterns, has been showing an important growth rate as a source and receiving region for tourism flows in this decade.

The present issue includes 9 relevant papers dealing with outstanding areas of interest at the level of tourism research, both from the professional and academic perspectives in the Ibero-American region. Topics covered are quite varied, including wine tourism initiatives rising in Mexico, cruise tourism analysis in Spain, the medical tourism in the Mexico–USA border, eco-tourism in Spain, sustainability indicators for mature destinations, or the role of urbanism in tourism planning and design among others. In more detail, the paper by Alicia García-Amaya, Rafael Temes-Cordovez, Moisés Simancas-Cruz, and María Pilar Peñarrubia deals with the role of urbanism in the tourism development, showing how urbanism can contribute to improve destination sustainability and planning. The contribution of Rosa María Shaadi-Rodríguez, Leticia Shaadi-Rodríguez, Ismael Rodríguez-Herrera, and Juan Ignacio Pulido-Fernández analyses the Magic Peoples´ Program in Mexico, identifying localities in involvement phase in the program and how these are positioned in terms of the destination life cycle stages. The article by Antonio García-Sánchez, David Siles-López, and María de Mar Vázquez-Méndez revisits the tourism competitiveness theory, showing how this concept influences the level of prosperity of the local populations by relying on innovation processes. The paper by Miguel Ángel Tobarra-González and Javier Mendoza Monpeán proposes a procedure and estimates the recreational value of El Valle and Carrascoy Natural Park in the Region of Murcia, Spain, by employing the Travel Cost Methodology.

The contribution of Belén Cobacho-Tornel defines and employs a new type of synthetic indicator to measure the sustainability of destinations, with an application for the coastal area in Murcia, Spain. The paper by Andrés Artal-Tur, José Miguel Navarro-Azorín, and José María Ramos-Parreño analyses the economic impact of cruise tourism by relying on improved Input–Output Tables developed for Spain at a regional level. They show how this methodology increases the accuracy of previous estimations. The article by Gerardo Novo and Maribel Osorio shows how the wine tourism industry is reaching a remarkable development in the last years in Mexico, in relation with the development of the tourism food-related industry. Also for Mexico, the contribution of María

Teresa Martínez-Almanza, Jaume Guía-Julve, Santos Alonso Morales-Muñoz, and Francisco Bribiescas-Silva presents the interesting case of medical border tourism that has been established in Ciudad Juárez, México with regards to their US neighbours. Finally, Beatriz Mayén-Cañavate, Juan Andrés Bernal-Conesa, Antonio Juan Briones-Peñalver, and Pedro Anunciação open an important debate on the relationship of the tourism sector and the marine resources regarding the Blue Growth Strategy recently launched by the European Commission. Along their paper, these authors propose a model for the management and integration of these resources in regards to Spain and Portugal.

In summary, this number presents a set of contributions to research and analysis of the current situation of the tourism sector for the whole Ibero-American world, including The Americas, Spain and Portugal. All papers come from researchers attending the last *9th ANATOLIA World Conference on Graduate Research in Tourism, Hospitality and Leisure* that took place in Cartagena, Spain, during the month of June 2017.

Andrés Artal-Tur and Antónia Correia

ORCID

Andrés Artal-Tur ⓘD http://orcid.org/0000-0003-3423-8570
Antónia Correia ⓘD http://orcid.org/0000-0002-6707-8289

Urban development and evolution of Valencian seaside destinations

Alicia M. García-Amaya, Rafael R. Temes-Cordovez, Moisés R. Simancas-Cruz and María Pilar Peñarrubia-Zaragoza

ABSTRACT

Mass tourism activity entails resource consumption and land uses usually difficult to be managed in a satisfactory way by urban planners. In practice, urbanism becomes a key tool in the design and conformation of tourist destinations, and, consequently, in their degree of success. This paper analyses the role of urbanism in the evolution of four relevant coastal destinations in the Valencian region in Spain. The aim of the research is to investigate the relationship between urban planning and tourist activity performance. Such an approach looks for opening a space of reflection for the scope of urbanism in helping destinations to achieve competitiveness and sustainability dimensions.

Introduction

Tourism activity, since its origin as mass phenomenon, has generated resource consumption and complexity of uses whose management has hardly been satisfactory addressed by urban planning. The main critics usually focus on the fact that there is no urbanism proper to tourism, but it had been imported – most times, in an uncritical way – from residential planning. On the other hand, the rush to develop most tourist destinations in the 1960s is often pointed as the main cause of a lack of reflection and abuse of the territory in these locations.

Urbanism has had, since the beginning of mass tourism phenomenon, an important role in generation and transformation of tourist destinations, their image, identity and capability to support tourist activity, and, consequently, in the degree of success of these locations in different periods and its adaptation for changing needs. This paper analyses the role of urbanism in the evolution of four relevant coastal tourist destinations in the Valencian Community (Spain): Peñíscola, Cullera, Denia and Altea. The research is based on the legal framework related to urbanism in different periods and the policies fostered by Public Administration that had influenced urban planning. It evaluates the results of urban planning as generating tourist destinations and its influence in development of tourist activity and residential tourism. The aim of this research is to highlight the relation between urban planning and tourist activity, in order to propel new reflections which help urbanism to propose solutions to make mature destinations and future developments in tourist sites be more competitive and sustainable.

Literature review

The evolution of sea and sun tourist destinations in Spain and, particularly, in the Valencian Community, has been widely addressed by scholars, due to the relevance of this kind of tourism in the GDP of this country and region. Urban planners and architects have underlined the difficulty to manage together questions as the demand of leisure and accommodation related to tourism, the profit expectations of implied agents, inhabitants' needs and other factors as landscape and resources preservation, that have not been satisfactorily addressed by urbanism in tourist destinations.

Furthermore, in the last 25 years, the use of "magic formulas" to renovate tourist destinations -such as golf resorts, leisure harbours, singular events or buildings-, has involved the homogenization of territory, disfavouring the competitiveness of tourist destinations (Vera, 2005). Several authors have presented, from different perspectives, the relationship between the urbanization phenomenon and tourism (Mazón, Huete, Mantecón, & Jorge, 2009; Vera & Marchena, 1995), the need of resources balance (Antón & Wilson, 2016; Vera & Baños, 2004) and the opportunity to foster the identity and the intrinsic values of tourist areas (Antón, 2010; Hernández, 2009; Silva, 2009), while proposing the integration of new activities and qualification strategies to renovate mature tourist destinations (Antón, 2004; Vera, 2005; Vera & Baños, 2010).

We maintain that urbanism has a very important role in the transformation of image and identity of tourist locations, so as its authenticity, which is key to guarantee their success as tourist destinations. In this context, urbanism contributes to modify the identity of tourist destinations, understanding the term "identity" as a re-presentation related to places intentionally projected by the different agents to reach the tourists (Marine, 2011, 2015).

Methodology

This research is based on a qualitative analysis of several parameters that have influenced the evolution of coastal tourist destinations. By an accurate selection of bibliography and sources, a general context for different periods has been established. Then, it has been made a case study of four coastal tourist destinations in the Valencian Community (Peñíscola, Cullera, Denia and Altea) since their origin as tourist recipients until the present time. A dynamic analysis has been carried out on the evolution of several factors over the last six decades:

- Features of these areas (landscape, land uses, heritage, culture, economy, demography, etc.) which are essential for the image and identity of tourist destinations, and its evolution since the 1960s decade until the present time.
- The response given from urban planning to meet the demands of tourist phenomenon, and the degree of accomplishment of planning previsions for urban development in those municipalities.
- Amount of homes built in different periods in those municipalities.
- Relationship between tourism, second homes and urban growth.
- Consequences of tourism on demography and employment in these locations.
- Presence of residential tourism and permanent residence of foreigners.
- Future projects planned for these areas (urban-planning).

For this research they have been analysed town plans and partial plans, aerial photographs and tourist brochures edited by Public Administration in different periods, cadastral and statistical data and specific literature.

Results

Attending to the legal framework, the origin of tourist cities in Spain and, in general, the residential estates that started to develop at the beginning of the tourist boom in Spain, were executed attending to the determinations of the Land Law approved in 1956. This national law was redacted in the 1950's decade, after a long period of international isolation that had kept the country in industrial and technological underdevelopment. It stated a rigid hierarchy of urban plans through which Public Administration established the final destination of the land, with the aim of ensuring the common good and rationalizing the process of urban develop-. ment. Those plans determined, as a right related to each portion of land, its use and building size. It also stated the duty to urbanize in order to build in urban land and land for development areas.

It became a hard task to process and approve urban plans. Slowness and rigidity of that processes, pressures from landowners – who willed higher profits – and malpractice executed by public agents were, in most cases, causes of poor quality in many urban plans designed in the 1960s and 1970s. Another relevant aspect is the fact that the Land Law did not state minimum urban standards, allowing to urban plans to set them freely. In addition, this law defined as building plots those urban land areas suitable for building and urbanizing according with the minimum standards set by urban plans. However, if plans had not defined those standards, it would only be necessary to have paved roadway, sidewalk curbs, tap water, sewerage system and street lighting to be considered as a building plot.

As a result, many buildings located along roads or boardwalks were built inside the borders of original agricultural plots, forcing their shapes to accomplish the urban standards set by plans. In most cases, the quality of the resultant living spaces was poor and the free areas of the plots were residual, being not suitable for placing sports facilities or swimming pools. Another consequence of the right to build along paved streets with minimum services was raise of buildings along the beachfront, even so the rear parts of their plots limited with agricultural land, agricultural paths or irrigation ditches.

It is important to underline that policies promoted by the government in the 1960s fostered urban growth of tourist destinations, so as increasing number of tourists went hand in hand with an increase in wealth of the regions. This idea propitiated all kind of abuses in development of areas qualified as tourist. In these locations, most spaces for leisure are private, so the lack of quality of urban spaces is even greater than in the rest of urban fabrics. The exceptions are the sea front promenades, where it is concentrated the activity which has to supply residential areas.

During the 1960s, the amount of land for sale increased considerably, whereas before then, land market was practically non-existent. Speculation had made sale of land became more profitable than its agricultural use. The Oil Crisis in the early 1970s was a brake on urban development which took more than a decade to retrieve, so many of the changes on regulations had little effects on tourist destinations during the following years. In the 1990's decade, Autonomous Communities in Spain acquired competence to regulate urbanism in their regions. The Valencian Community approved the LRAU (Law 6/1994 that regulated the urbanism activity). A key aspect of this law was that it provided more flexibility in urban processes, so it gave ability to lower rank plans (such as partial plans) to modify upper rank ones (Town Plans), in order to meet the changing needs of society.

The LRAU not only introduced the concept of equal distribution of benefits and burdens in land for development, but also set urban standards such as building size limitation, or a minimum reserve of land for public services and facilities such as green areas in future land developments. The result was a kind of urbanism formed by small self-sufficient urban cores in which a global vision of territory is missed, as urban space suitable to meet the needs of citizens.

The law that substituted the LRAU, the Law 16/2005, of Valencian development law (LUV), started to be applied in 2006, less than two years before the first effects of the global crisis were noticed. However, it was approved in an especially overdevelopment period, so this law had a big impact, due to the application of its rules for Integrated Actions Programmes (PAI) and Isolated Actions Programmes (PAA). The main innovation of these procedures involved the fact that the approval of those programmes could be simultaneous to the approval of partial plans of their areas. That way, it was possible to quickly urbanize areas of urban land and land for development even if there was not a previous detailed design of urban fabric set by town-plans. Similarly, with Isolated Actions Programmes, many buildings were raised together with the services that gave them the right to be built. This kind of actuations permitted the progressive and fast expansion of urban fabrics in tourist and holiday locations between 2006 and 2008.

By contrast, the law 5/2014 of land planning, urbanism and landscape protection (LOTUP) that substituted the LUV, has had little influence on the processes of development of the tourist destinations, so that it was approved in a context of breakdown of the real estate market, which is recovering at present.

Summarizing, urban fabrics in tourist locations have become traditionally the result of a mix of individual interests and rights determined by urban plans and laws, so as willingness of increasing tourist accommodation capacity, fostered by government policies. That framework has provoked lack of public space and facilities in coastal tourist areas, which is necessary to implement in order to maintain and propel quality of tourist destinations.

Case study

Tourist areas in the analysed municipalities are examples of the territorial evolution of many municipalities in the Valencian Community. Although every municipality has been developed according to their pre-existences and under the conditions set by their town-plans over decades, the conclusions generated about urban spaces can be extended to other tourist destinations. The Table 1 shows similarities and contrasts in urban development of the four analyzed municipalities, which are explained in the following paragraphs.

Morphological and use analysis

Related to this research, the types of tourist-residential settlements could be distinguished as follows: Second homes developments in the coastal strip, mixed-uses developments in the coastal strip, and second homes developments in slopes with sea views. The first type of settlements are second homes developments with high-rise buildings, or combining high-rise buildings with single-family homes. These buildings generally have private common facilities such as sports grounds, swimming pools or playgrounds for children. In these locations, there are important

Table 1. Resume of similarities and contrasts in the urban development of Peñíscola, Cullera, Denia and Altea (1959–1917).

Similarities	Contrasts
• Existence of previous urban plans. • Large authorized construction volumes	• Size of the plots and authorized features for buildings have consequences in the use of houses as principal dwellings, second homes and as recipients of residential tourism.
• Proliferation of second homes. • Persistence of agricultural plots. • Oversize of areas for development alongside the coastline, but construction only in the seafront. • Lack of appreciation of agricultural land. • Search of immediate profit. • Popular reception of the planned actions because of the multiplicity of land owners. • Multiplicity of individual actions instead cohesive development.	• Processing plans: Designed before the economic crisis: oversize of areas for development next to the coastline and in mountain slopes with sea views. Designed after the burst of the real estate bubble: protection of natural and agricultural values by banning the urbanization of singular areas where precedent plans authorized housing.

lacks of public spaces, and shops concentrate along the seafront promenade or in certain blocks. Many buildings are located inside their plots without any contact with the streets, so that no commercial space can be set in their ground floor. Most homes built in these areas are designed as second homes, even so, over the last two decades they have started to be used as main homes. However, there is an important lack of services proper of residential areas. Business such those related to leisure time, restaurants and seasonal activities prevail over daily shopping ones. This type of business remains closed during the most part of the year.

The second type – mixed-uses developments in the coastal strip –, combines blocks of apartments with hotels and other kinds of tourist accommodation. Similarly to the model explained before, these developments have a lack of services and the existing ones usually are seasonal, even in those areas certain tourist activity remains during the whole year, such as the North beach of Peñíscola.

The third type of settlements, second homes developments in slopes with sea views, are usually formed by detached houses or villas with different plot sizes and, sometimes, hotel buildings or public equipment are included in these areas. In these residential estates, size of plots has been key to determine the use of dwellings as seasonal or permanent. Detached houses included in urban developments of the 1970s and 1980s consisting in small plots, have maintained their use as second homes. On contrast, those developments in which the minimum plot set by plans has been considerably wide – for instance, in most locations of Altea –, dwellings have been used as main homes since their construction. Size of plots has also influenced residential tourism, which started in the late 1990s. According to this, residential estates with large plots have been preferred by foreigners to establish their main residences or to stay for long periods during the year.

Chronological development of urbanization and buildings

Even existing some exceptions such as Cerromar or Capblanc estates in Peñíscola, – where many houses were built years before public infrastructure was finished – most dwellings located in slopes were built after the approval of the partial plans and the execution of the development projects related to their estates. However, the most part of coastal areas have been developed into strips parallel to the coast line. This has occurred even in places where the town-plans had previously defined wide areas of urban soil. In these cases, many buildings have raised along a pre-existent street, before the development of the area took place. It has occurred because of the legitimacy of building if one of the sides of the plot is adjacent to a paved street with minimum services, or, after the approval of the LUV, according to Isolated or Integrated Actions Programmes.

The results of this have been buildings involved (excepting for their main façade) in agricultural land. Another feature of these buildings is that they are included in plots that keep the limits of the agricultural land plots, not following a logical division according to the urban blocks designed by town-plans. A consequence of these actions is an irregular urban border that follows the agricultural plots limits, what is not the most appropriate for the resultant buildings, and will condition the form of the buildings that will be constructed in adjacent plots. The Figure 1 shows the sequence of building in different areas of the analyzed municipalities. It can be observed how the preexisting borders of the agricultural plots have conditioned the shape and position of buildings and streets in some areas of Peñíscola and Denia.

Services

Aspects related to the design of urban fabrics, such as the fact of not having followed the logical sequence of urban development – urban planning, management of acting programmes, urbanization and building processes – have been the main causes of the lack of services in the analysed tourist destinations. In the Figure 2 it can be appreciated the lack of services and retail areas. It is

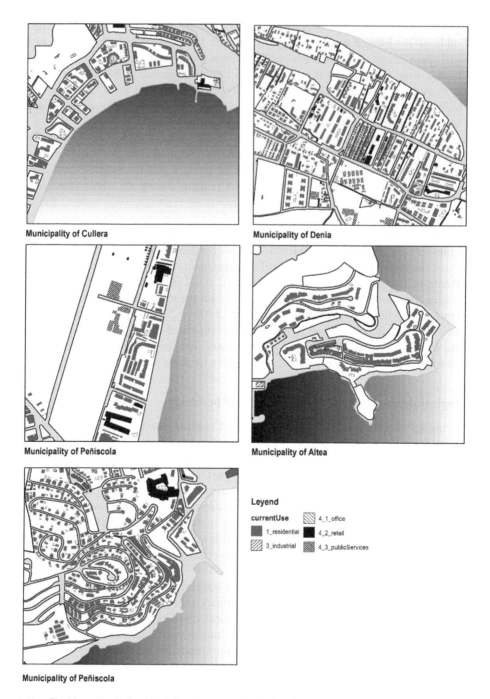

Figure 1. Use of buildings. Detail of residential/tourist areas in Peñíscola, Cullera, Denia and Altea. Prepared by the authors on PNOA images. Sources: Instituto Geográfico Nacional of Spain. Dirección General del Catastro of Spain.

missed the providence of these services by the town-plans and the development programmes. This lack of services and public space cause difficulty in using the dwellings of these areas as main homes. The seasonal use of dwellings in many areas contrast on the continuous public expenditure for street lighting or garbage collection.

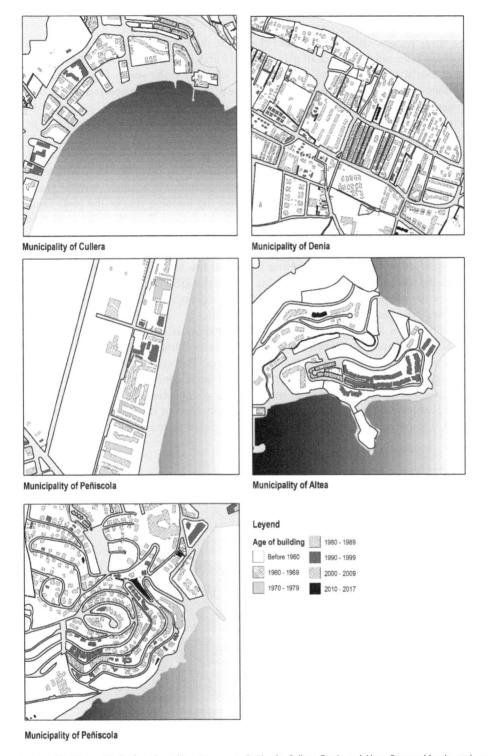

Figure 2. Age of buildings. Detail of residential/tourist areas in Peñíscola, Cullera, Denia and Altea. Prepared by the authors on PNOA images. Sources: Instituto Geográfico Nacional of Spain. Dirección General del Catastro of Spain.

Town-plans analysis

The case study focuses on the so repeated claim that the negative results of urbanism in tourist locations have been caused by lack of planning and hurry to perform different actions to meet the demand of tourist accommodation. It is proper to say that, in the years of tourist boom, it was a rush to obtain profit from tourism fostered by some policies but, in the analysed areas, most urban developments had been based on urban plans previously approved or permitted by them. Generally, the town-plan (P.G.O.U.) of a municipality is developed through partial and urbaniza- tion plans but, in some cases, the partial plans had been approved first, and then the P.G.O.U. was designed involving all the partial plans which were in process at that moment.

It can be stated that local plans based on the Land Law, 1956, permitted large building volumes, due to the fact that this law did not set urban standards. Building volumes were, in practice, only limited by functional reasons, in order not to affect the building size of the plots around. The analysis of the evolution of urbanization in the studied locations show that, although urban plans had provided and, in some cases, even defined coherent urban fabrics, in practice, the process of building was developed into strips parallel to the coast line. This fact, added to the oversize of the areas to build set by these overdeveloping plans, are the basis of the urbanism bad results in Spanish coastal tourist destinations. According to that, the main cause of these results was the lack of strategies to assure a progressive and coherent development of the territory and protect landscape and resources from private short-term profit.

Another common feature in the analysed municipalities is the fact that, under the pretext of tourism, large areas were developed and destined to second homes (flats or villas), even most of them were not expected to be acquired by foreigners. The conditions set by the urban plans (minimum plot, maximum buildability, etc.) have had direct consequences on the use of houses as principal dwellings or second homes, as well as on the phenomenon of residential tourism. In the Figure 3 it is shown the progressive growth of the built areas in the four analyzed municipalities since 1959. The overdevelopment of second homes related to tourism destinations is key in the

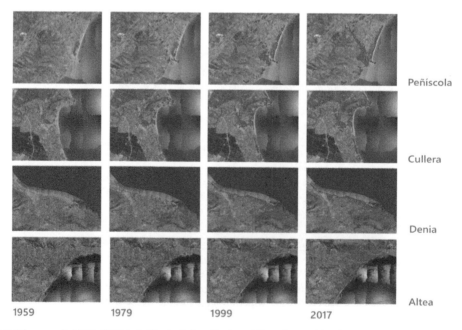

Figure 3. Urban growth (1959–2016) in Peñíscola, Cullera, Denia and Altea. Prepared by the authors on PNOA maps. Sources: Instituto Geográfico Nacional of Spain. Dirección General del Catastro of Spain.

seasonal use of most part of the territory and have conditioned the social and economic structures of these areas so as the perception of the landscape.

In general, the plans processing nowadays which have been designed before the current economic crisis, replicate overdevelopment of the plans approved in the decades of 1960 and 1970. They do not try to solve the problems of built areas but generate more land for development where start from zero. In overdeveloping periods, there were two constant factors that helped to justify the change of agricultural use of plots to provide large areas for development: a low economic and cultural appreciation of agricultural land and landowners' wish to obtain immediate profit. These reasons, added to the multiplicity of landowners in coastal areas, have traditionally motivated the support for plans and policies which fostered overdevelopment. All of this has been the cause of the current existence of an important stock of unoccupied houses, which has not easily been absorbed by real-estate market.

The processing General Urban Plan (P.G.O.U) of Altea – designed after the burst of the real estate bubble – shows a change of strategy which can be the beginning of a brake for overdevelopment. It do not address the problem of management of agricultural landscape preservation or private buildings, but it is the first step towards a future in which urban regeneration, landscape and heritage preservation will be more present in urban planning of tourist locations.

Comparative analysis of the housing stock

Urban model, location and features of dwellings, intensity of building activity and age of buildings are closely related to the character of each municipality, its growth expectations and activity, and must be the basis for more sustainable growth patterns adjusted to the citizens' needs. Through the analysis of social and tourist context, and the proportion of main dwellings, second and vacant homes and number of inhabitants, the current framework of each municipality can be explained, in order to obtain some criteria for projecting their future transformations.

Peñíscola has 7,413 inhabitants (according to 2017 data from the National Statistics Office of Spain, INE) and, in the last census of dwellings dated in 2011, there was a stock of 16,802 dwellings. It mains a ratio of 2.26 dwellings per inhabitant. Only the 19.31% of these dwellings were main homes, 49.97% were second homes and the rest (30.72%) were vacant. Cullera, which has much larger population – 21,999 inhabitants (2017) – had in 2011 a stock of 28,986 dwellings (1.32 dwellings per inhabitant). 31.62% of them were main homes, 27.99% were second homes and only 10.39% kept vacant. Altea, which has a population similar to Cullera's (21,813 inhabitants in 2017), had a stock of 16,430 dwellings in 2011 (0.75 dwellings per inhabitant). A total of 55.30% of the global were main homes, 23.63 would be second homes and the remaining 21.07% would be vacant. Finally, Denia, the municipality with the largest population of those analysed –41,568 inhabitants in 2017 –, had in 2011 a stock of 43,342 dwellings (1.04 dwellings per inhabitant). A total of 39.8% of them were main homes, 28.8% second homes and 31.35% would be vacant.

The differences of the related data could be explained as follows:

Denia and Cullera have more diversified economic bases, effect that, in the case of Cullera, is maximized by its proximity to Valencia City. Both are municipalities with a ratio of dwellings per inhabitant close to 1. However, the difference between the amount of second homes and vacant ones in both municipalities is quite significant. The figures of vacant dwellings in Cullera are especially low, due to the age of buildings, since the main urban development took place in the 1970s and 1980s. In fact, building activity in Denia was very intense during the 1980s, 1990s and the early 2000s. The most active decade for real estate market in this municipality was the period 1997–2006, in which 16,502 dwelling were built (it means the 38% of the total stock of dwellings registered in 2011). Building activity in Denia remained up to 2008, even then it suffered an important decrease, stopping almost completely in 2010.

Altea is the one of the analysed municipalities which has the highest percentage of main homes, greater than 50%, even the most part of its dwelling stock is constituted by villas. The cause of this permanent use of dwellings in Altea is related to the fact that 31% of its population are foreign people, many of them retired. It is also important, in these municipality, the phenomenon known as residential tourism, constituted by foreigners that stay large periods during the year in their second homes. Even residential tourism is not directly reflected in the statistics of use of dwellings, it is a fact that a great part of second homes in Altea have an annual occupancy rate much higher than in other municipalities, where second homes are occupied only during the summer season. All of this is maximized by the goodness of the climate conditions of that location, which are attractive to residential use, and favour tourist activity over a large part of the year.

On contrast, the climate conditions of Peñíscola are not so suitable for tourist activity or residential use during the winter months, even so there remains certain tourist activity, especially on weekends. The basis of the Peñíscola's activity is related to tourism and services which, even remaining during all the year, still have a strong seasonal character. In fact, the population of Peñíscola raises significantly during the summer months, due to the ammount of the second homes and hotel occupancy (Peñíscola has 8,586 places in hotels, which is 16% more than the registered population of the municipality, according to 2017 data). These facts cause, moreover, the coming of an important number of seasonal workers which, added to the local labour force, fill the labour market destined to serve to tourist and vacationers. Most of these workers stay in rented dwellings, different to those demanded by tourists, which remain unoccupied during the periods of lower tourist activity.

Building activity in Peñíscola was developed especially in the 1980s decade, even there was a second period, between 1998 and 2007, in which more than 7,000 dwellings were built, which represent the 43.3% of the total stock (according to 2011 census). The economic crisis starting in 2007 is the main cause that an important number of dwellings (new and used ones) have remained vacant, due to the high prices that – despite the effects of the economic crisis – have been characterising the real estate market in this municipality. Special mention should be made of houses located at the Historical Centre of Peñíscola which, due to their singularity and location, have especially high prizes that contrast with their lack of maintenance and poor living conditions. These dwellings remain, in a significant rate, vacant during the most part of the year. Even so, their rentals provide important profits to their owners during the summer season.

Foreign populations

Since 2001–2012, a raising trend of permanent residence of foreign people occurs in some locations at the Costa Blanca and other coastal municipalities in the Community of Valencia. In Denia and Altea, British and German colonies are especially large. However, in 2013 a sudden fall of foreign population occurred in the analysed municipalities, excepting for Cullera. A significant part of the diminished population is British and German, especially in the municipalities of Alicante, where those colonies are greater. On contrast, de variation of the Spanish population is insignificant in the four studied municipalities.

The decrease of the number of permanent foreigner residents in the analysed municipalities is a recent data, but the trend has remained over the last four years. It is necessary to make a wider study to see if that trend affects to a large number of tourist destinations or if they are punctual phenomena. Furthermore, there are no official data related to the decrease of residential tourists, which are the foreigner that are not registered as residents but stay in their second homes during large periods in the year. Huete, Mantecón, and Estévez (2013) have addressed the impact of the economic crisis on the mobility of foreigner residents in Spain and especially in the province of Alicante (Mantecón, Huete, & Estévez; 2013) but it would be necessary to research more thoroughly possible effects of this trend and propose strategies to renovate and return attractiveness to mature destinations.

Conclusion and implications

The aim of this paper has been to analyse how urbanism has influenced the generation and transformation of four relevant coastal tourist destinations in the Valencian Community (Spain), as urban, territorial and tourist models. The results of this analysis could be useful as basis to forecast consequences of urban planning decisions in future tourist models as well as in regeneration of mature coastal tourist destinations.

The research made has revealed that many urban dysfunctions occurred in sun and sea mature destinations have been related to the difficulty of urban planning to manage a proper sequence of land development. Other causes of dysfunctions have been caused by the lack of minimum urban standards which guaranteed the quality of urban spaces and facilities and by the individual interests of landowners to achieve the greatest profits as possible. Furthermore, urban planning has had a big influence in seasonality of tourist areas, use of dwellings as main or second homes and residential tourism phenomenon.

The research concludes that urban regeneration is not only necessary for tourist destinations that started to develop in the 60s and 70s of the last century – which can be involved in a process of obsolescence –, but also for those which have been developed recently without the proper equipment and with spontaneous urbanization borders. It is necessary to unite all these areas with the rest of the territory and provide them with quality of life, identity, functionality and diversity of tourist activities, through the analysis of the lacks and needs of every of them. The final objective for urbanism in tourist destinations could be to establish a proper urban planning to generate flexible and sustainable urban models, which could meet the changing needs of inhabitants and tourists.

Acknowledgements

This research is part of the Project "Analysisis of urban sustainability as a strategy for regeneration of public space of coastal tourist areas", funded by the Caja Canarias Foundation and managed by the Vice-rectorate of Research of the Universidad de La Laguna, Spain [Grant id: 2017REC17]. It is also funded by the Project "Crisis and Restructuring of tourist areas of the Spanish Coast" [Grant id: CSO2015-64468-P], Ministry of Economy, Industry and Competitiveness (MINECO), Spain.

Disclosure statement

No potential conflict of interest was reported by the authors.

Funding

This work was supported by the Caja Canarias Foundation and Vice-rectorate of Research of the Universidad de La Laguna, Spain [Grant id: 2017REC17]. It was also supported by Ministry of Economy, Industri and Competitiveness (MINECO) [Grant id: CSO2015-64468-P].

References

Antón, S. (2004). De los procesos de diversificación y cualificación a los productos turísticos emergentes. Cambios y oportunidades en la dinámica reciente del turismo litoral [Diversification and requalifying of emerging tourism products]. *Papeles De Economía Española, 102*, 316–333.

Antón, S. (2010). Identitat i turisme. Entre la imatge i la percepció [Identity and tourism, between image and perception]. *Paradigmes: Economia Productiva I Coneixement, 5*, 156–165.

Anton, S., & Wilson, J. (2016). The evolution of coastal tourism destinations: A path plasticity perspective on tourism urbanisation. *Journal of Sustainable Tourism, 25*(1), 96–112.

Hernández. (2009). M. El paisaje como seña de identidad territorial: Valorización social y factor de desarrollo, ¿utopía o realidad? [Landscape as a territorial identity sign]. *Boletín De La Asociación De Geógrafos Españoles, 49*, 169–183.

Huete, R., Mantecón, A., & Estévez, J. (2013). Challenges in lifestyle migration research: Reflections and findings about the Spanish crisis. *Mobilities, 8*(3), 331–348.

Mantecón, A., Huete, R., & Estévez, J. (2013). El impacto de la crisis económica sobre la movilidad internacional de los residentes extranjeros en la provincia de Alicante [The impact of economic crisis on international mobility of foreign residents in the province of Alicante]. *Revista Internacional De Estudios Migratorios, 3*(2), 155–184.

Marine, E. (2011). The Image and identity of the Catalan coast as a tourist destination in twentieth-century tourist guidebooks. *Journal of Tourism and Cultural Change, 9*(2), 118–139.

Marine, E. (2015). Identity and authenticity in destination image construction. *Anatolia: an International Journal of Tourism and Hospitality Research, 26*(4), 574–587.

Mazón, T., Huete, R., Mantecón, A., & Jorge, E. (2009). Legitimación y crisis en la urbanización de las regiones turísticas mediterráneas [Legitimation and crisis in the urbanization process of tourism mediterranean regions]. In T. Mazón, R. Y. M. Huete, & Alejandro (Eds.), *Turismo, urbanización y estilos de vida. Las nuevas formas de la movilidad residencial* (pp. 399–412). Barcelona: Icaria.

Silva Pérez, R. (2009). Agricultura, paisaje y patrimonio territorial: Los paisajes de la agricultura vistos como patrimonio [Agriculture, landscape and territorial heritage]. *Boletín De La Asociación De Geógrafos Españoles, 49*, 309–334.

Vera, J. F. (2005). El auge de la función residencial en destinos turísticos del litoral mediterráneo: Entre el crecimiento y la renovación [The rise of the residential use in the mediterranean seaside destinations]. *Papers De Turisme, 37*, 95–116.

Vera, J. F., & Baños, C. J. (2004). Turismo, territorio y medio ambiente. La necesaria sostenibilidad [Tourism, territory and the environment. The necessary sustainable dimension]. *Papeles De Economía Española, 102*, 271–286.

Vera, J. F., & Baños, C. J. (2010). Renovación y reestructuración de los destinos turísticos consolidados del litoral: Las prácticas recreativas en la evolución del espacio turístico [Renovation and restructuring of consolidated tourism seaside destinations]. *Boletín De La Asociación De Geógrafos Españoles, 53*, 329–353.

Vera, J.F. & Marchena, M (1995). Promoción inmobiliaria y configuración de la oferta turística [Real estate market and the tourim supply side] in Assotiation Internationale d'Experts Scientifiques du Tourisme (ed.), Rapports 45 Congrès de la AIEST (Vol.3, pp. 29-51), St. Gallen.

Magic peoples programme – its localities in phase of involvement

Rosa María Angélica Shaadi Rodríguez, Leticia del Socorro Shaadi Rodríguez, Juan Ignacio Pulido-Fernández⬤ and Ismael Manuel Rodríguez Herrera

ABSTRACT
The central target of this investigation has been to identify localities in the involvement phase inside its life cycle like destinations Magic Town, pointing out the characteristics that they possess in this stage based on the model of the life cycle of Butler. The methodology was based on the analysis of the diagnoses elaborated by the Ministry of Tourism of Mexico for the Magic Villages, in which there were examined variables of competitiveness and sustainability, which provided information relating to the characteristics of the life cycle. The results reveal that localities in this involvement phase present characteristics together related to the inflow, the seasonal nature, types of attractions, the connectivity and the scarce rendering of tourist service.

Introduction

In the last years, the tourist activity has received such importance in the world, which has revealed its transcendency, on having contributed varied benefits to the destinations that have taken refuge in her. This in turn, it has allowed to the tourism to grow in a continuous way, generating that other places and communities are interested by its promotion. At present, the tourism is considered to be a catalyst of local economic growth, a promoter of the conservation of the cultural identity of peoples and an agent transformer in the social progress of these, by why an increasing number of diverse localities, they examine its potential in resources of attraction, of services and of infrastructure, which allow them to penetrate into the tourism development.

The Federal Ministry of Tourism of Mexico institutes in 2001, the Magic Peoples Program of Mexico for the purpose of the tourist offer of the country diversifies and to recognize and to value the cultural and natural wealth of populations, who, due to it are provided with a potentiality for the tourist development. Ministry of Tourism (2014a) defines to this federal programme of the following way: "The Magic Peoples Program of Mexico is an integral tourist development programme of the Ministry of Tourism, for localities that, in a different developmental level, organize diverse actions of economic, social and environmental character with the intention of improving the living conditions of a tourist locality" (p. 4). In turn, the programme provides also, the definition of Magic Village: "A Magic Village is a locality that has symbolic attributes, legends, history, transcendent facts and routine character, anyway magic that comes in each of its cultural declarations and that they mean today, a big opportunity for the tourist use". (Ministry of Tourism, 2014a, p. 4)

Being rural and semirural communities of the country, which, on having been incorporated into this federal programme, receive support, promotion and recognition to penetrate into the development of the tourism, like an innovative activity for them, they need to know what is the evolution that they are achieving in its status as tourist destination, so that one could consider in the plans and municipal programmes of tourist development, the establishment of targets that should allow them to achieve an effective reality in its condition of receiving communities of tourism, under the categorization that grants them the Magic Peoples Program of Mexico. Thus it has been adopted like reference frame to realize an evolutionary analysis in these localities, the model of the Life Cycle of the Tourist Destinations proposed by Butler (1980), since this theory proposes for every stage of life of any type of tourist destination, those circumstances that will allow to identify the progress that these communities are conquering in the field of the tourist activity.

The central target of this investigation, has been to be located to localities that find in the involvement phase inside its life cycle like destinations Magic Village, identifying, from it, the main peculiarities that they have in common for being placed in this stage, as well as other characteristics that they possess and that will allow them to advance towards the development stage in the life cycle model. Based on this target, the results of this investigation will contribute to: (1) evaluate the situation and gradually of advance of these localities as tourist destinations, (2) value the realized actions proposed in a tourist planning of the destination as Magic Village, (3) face efforts those allow to strengthen the obtained achievements and generate new advance perspectives, and (4) propitiate the conditions, which thus allow an effective tourist management of these destinations.

Literature review

The improving of a destination in the ambience of the tourism, it is achieved based on the knowledge that it is had on the conditions under which its progress happens, to generate advantages that allow him to reach an effective competitiveness on the tourist market. To go so far as to have this knowledge, it is necessary to realize a diagnosis that shows the local general or specific situation. One of the instruments of major use to diagnose the evolution of a destination with base in certain characteristics, independently of the type of tourism that in him is carried out, is the model of life cycle of tourist destinations proposed by Butler in the 80s (Choy, 1992; Cooper & Jackson, 1989; France, 1991; García, 2011; Hovinen, 2002; Pérez & Páez, 2014; Virgen, 2009).

The model of the life cycle of Butler (1980), has been a tool used to analyze different perspectives or approaches in the tourist destinations: to measure the competitive diversity that these places present with regard to its stage of life (García, Reinares, & Armelini, 2013; Gonçalves-Gândara, Domareski, Chim, & Biz, 2013; Pike, 2009; Soares, Gândara, & Ivars, 2012), or to evaluate the dynamics of change and historical development in the destination inside the tourist ambience (Digance, 1997; Garay & Cànoves, 2011; Ngaire, 1997; Schuckert, Möller, & Weiermair, 2007), or to diversify or to restructure the local tourist offer, taking this model as instrument of prediction or description (Agarwal, 2002; Hovinen, 2002; Montaño, Pérez, & De la O, 2014; Pérez & Páez, 2014; Schuckert et al., 2007; Vera & Baños, 2010).

This life cycle model has been considered to be a good theoretical contribution that can go so far as to have effectiveness on having complemented itself with other approaches or models (Digance, 1997; Garay & Cànoves, 2011) that make it more flexible and practical to be able to take into consideration other factors that influence the life and competitiveness of the tourist destinations (García, 2011; Gonçalves-Gândara et al., 2013; Hovinen, 2002; Oreja, Parra, & Yanes, 2008; Ritchie & Crouch, 2000). Inside the life cycle of a tourist destination, every stage possesses its own characteristics (Butler, 1980). But also it must be considered that different external and internal factors can exist, that they can affect the development of the phases of its life cycle, generating certain peculiarities (Soares et al., 2012) that need of a favourable treatment. The implementation of appropriate and effective strategies in the management of the destination, they will help to coordinate the previous thing, supporting with it the advance in its life cycle, as well as its competitiveness and position (González & Mendieta, 2009; Jiménez & Aquino, 2012; Ritchie & Crouch, 2003).

Life cycle

The model of life cycle of the tourist destination, shows the evolution of this one in the time across six stages (Figure 1), turning into an instrument of analysis that allows to know the tourist prosperity of a destination by means of the periodical arrivals of visitors (Butler, 1980).

Butler (1980) points out that this model continues the scheme of the concept of the cycle of the product, where the sales tend in a beginning to grow, later to became stable and finally to droop. Buhalis (2000) recounts that its main utility is to help to understand the development of destinations and to supply a guide that contributes to the capture of strategic decisions. But, when the information or sufficient information do not exist, it can there turns limited the use of this model as a descriptive instrument of the situation of the destination. Six stages suggested by Butler (1980) for the model of life cycle of tourist destinations, appear in the Table 1, showing in a synthetic way, the main characteristics of each one.

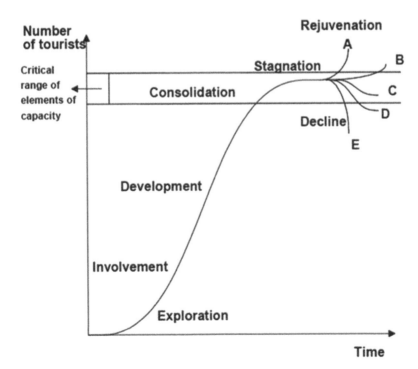

Figure 1. Hypothetical evolution of a tourist destination.
Source: Butler (1980).

Table 1. Characteristics of the stages of the life cycle of a tourist destination.

Stage	Characteristics
Exploration	- Most of occasional visitor. - Attractions designed like tourist offer do not exist. - Few connectivity.
Involvement	- Periods of tourist inflow begin to be identified. - Positive but slow tourist arrivals. -The use of attractions begins to be formalized. -The residents begin to take part in the services provision. - Access routes begin to develop.
Development	-The tourists' quantity in high periods can be equal or bigger than the population. -The attractions they trade in specific and with better facilities. -Perceptible changes in the physical appearance of the area. -Authorities and businessmen invest intensely in publicity. -Growth and progress in the accessibility.
Consolidation	-The visitors increase, but it diminishes the growth rate. -Whole of visitors overcomes to the whole of resident population. -Tourist products were content with the local tourist attractions. -Part of the local economy is tied to the tourism. -Tourist services are offered across exemption and chains. -Favourable transformation of the urban image. -The publicity performs wide scope. -Wide connectivity.
Stagnation	-The maximum visitors' inflow was reached. -Strong dependence on repetition of visits or of events that generate inflow. -The genuine natural and cultural attractions will be replaced with "artificial" facilities. -Capacity levels will have excelled themselves in diverse variables, creating different problems. -There will be surpluses in quarters offer. -The urban image will be complex. -Image well positioned but that will not be already fashionable.
Decline	-The tourists will not be already attracted; the destination will be used increasingly for weekend or trips of one day. -The area will not be capable of competing with the new attractions. -It will face a market in regression. -Disappearance of tourist facilities that do less attractive to the destination. -A gradual declination can happen up to coming to the entire slope or there can happen a stabilization that leads to a growth induced up to coming to rejuvenation.

Source: proper making from Butler (1980).

Methodology

This investigation is a study with scope of descriptive type in that one tries to identify the characteristics of the localities Magic Village in involvement phase inside its life cycle like tourist destinations.

Methodological exposition

The study is of not experimental type, since the information about the main characteristics of the life cycle of the localities of the sample, it is obtained in secondary sources. The analysis unit was the localities incorporated into the Magic Peoples Program of Mexico, of the Ministry of Tourism of Mexico. The population considered for the study there are 83 localities, of the 111 that exist at present, of which the Ministry of Tourism realized in 2014, the Diagnoses of Competitiveness and Sustainability of the Magic Peoples (Ministry of Tourism, 2014b).

One worked with a sample probabilistic random stratified, so that all the populations with this appointment had opportunity equality to be chosen, there being used like strata five regions (North, Gulf, Pacific Ocean, Centre and South) in which the Federal Ministry of Tourism across the Council of Tourist Promotion of Mexico (CPTM), has divided to the national territory, so that the populations could be located by major accuracy. With a maximum error of 10% and a wished level of confidence of 90%, extracting to him the sample of 83 localities of the population, this one decided using the programme STATS and its random selection was carried out also by means of the above mentioned programme. The sample remained shaped by 39 localities: 9 of the North region, 3 of the region of the Gulf of Mexico, 8 of the region Pacific Ocean, 16 of the Central region and 3 of the South region.

Information compilation

The Diagnoses of Competitiveness and Sustainability of the Magic Peoples were the main consulted secondary source, since they contain the information sufficient and updated to achieve the central target of this investigation, on having been documents generated by the Ministry of Tourism of the Federal Government. These documents are provided with scientific rigor, since its design was a not experimental descriptive and transeccional investigation, carried out with the involvement of the State and Local Governments responsible for the conduction of the tourist sector and of Institutions of Higher Education, to assure the quality of the same ones.

The Diagnoses of Competitiveness and Sustainability of the Magic Peoples were prepared based on the methodology indicated by the Ministry of Tourism, in which there was requested the study of 61 variables grouped in the competitiveness dimensions and sustainability that in turn, were subdividing in its respective attention areas. They were used like skills of compilation of information: direct compilation of federal, state and municipal entities; documentary review in State and Municipal Files; you interview local businessmen; you poll visitors; groups of approach and forums of consultation. Although there was used a methodology unified for the making of these diagnoses, the content and the composition of the information it was presented in accordance with the existing information and in the particular form of those who prepared the reports.

Work methodology

To shape the characterization of the stages of the life cycle of the localities study object, firstly, carried out the compilation of the Diagnoses on Competitiveness and Sustainability of the Magic Peoples of the sample to be able to realize later the analysis of the information that they contain. With base in the analyzed information there were outlined the characteristics of the life cycle of every territory, from the characteristics delineated by Butler (1980). Later, there was prepared a table in which there appear the localities detected in phase of involvement, grouped by region and with its year of incorporation to the programme, as well as the characteristics that distinguish them for being in this life stage. Finally, there were grouped the characteristics that have in common the localities in involvement stage, concentrating also, other characteristics identified by means of the analysis of the information and that belong to a later phase of the life cycle.

Results

Of the 39 localities that shaped the sample for this study, 16 of them (41, 02%) find in implication phase as for its life cycle like tourist destinations Magic Village. The Table 2 gathers the percentage corresponding to the quantity mistrial for region, in which there are, located each of the 16 localities that have been located in this stage of the life cycle.

The results that Table 2 presents allow to observe that the region with major populations quantity in implication phase is the region of the Gulf of Mexico, where its localities have between 7 and 10 years of having being incorporated into this programme and even present initial characteristics that could already have excelled to achieve an advance to another stage in its existence like Magic Peoples. On the other hand, the remaining regions, they present percentages that show that they are a less populations quantity in this stage, which can be an indicative of that a major number of localities, of the entire number that has every region, already finds in an advance situation as for its life cycle like destinations

Table 2. Magic Peoples in phase of involvement by regions.

Region	Entire quantity of Magic Peoples for region	Number of localities of the sample for stratum	Number of Magic Peoples identified in stage of involvement	Percentage for region with regard to the sample (%)
North	18	9	2	22,22
Gulf of Mexico	6	3	3	100
Pacific Ocean	17	8	4	50
Central	35	16	6	37,5
South	7	3	1	33,33
	N = 83	n = 39	16	

Magic Village. Table 3 shows the characteristics of the localities incorporated into the Magic Peoples Program of Mexico that were located in the involvement stage in its life cycle.

As soon as the characteristics of every population was identified based on the proposals by the model of the life cycle of Butler (1980), those common characteristics concentrated in these localities in the phase of involvement, which are listed next:

- It has not identified tourist periods or of visitors' inflow in the localities of the sample. Only in two of 16 populations (San Sebastian del Oeste, Jalisco and Real de Asientos, Aguascalientes) identified the summer and the Holy Week, like inflow periods.
- 75% of the localities has positive tourists arrivals in the year, and although concrete information does not exist on the persons' quantity that they visit to these localities, the arrivals they think in a wide status that it ranges between the 15,000 and 24,000 persons annually. Only in some localities, the arrivals quantities are reduced being estimated between 2000 and 5000 persons.
- Although there are a variety of attractive in these Magical Villages, natural resources are those that present greater use by different programmed activities in them, among which hiking, observation of species, abseiling, rock climbing, rappelling, camps and water activities, among others. It was identified that cultural attractions are lacking in use, because there is not a schedule of activities that the visitor can perform on them.
- The rendering of service, offered to tourists on the part of the residents, is incipient and even scarce or insufficient. Few tourist services in these localities neither present quality standards nor of professionalization in those who provide them.
- The connectivity exists in all these communities, being principally of terrestrial type. A total of 25% of these, catalogues its connectivity as good and sufficient, while 37.5% classifies it like reduced and 18.75% considers having an incipient terrestrial connectivity. Only 18.75% of these localities the possibilities of connectivity have begun to increase, by means of the construction ways that extend the step along terrestrial route or that allow the accessibility to the existing airport infrastructure in nearby municipalities.

As part of the target of this study, also there was examined the profile of the localities in the phase of involvement, for the purpose of finding the possible existence of other characteristics not belonging to this stage of the model of the life cycle. In a little more than half of 16 localities identified in this phase (56.25%), there were findings regarding certain peculiarities that although they are evident in an incipient way, begin already to appear like strategies that impel the tourist growth of these populations towards a development stage. These finds are listed next.

- In 68.75% of the localities there has been detected the use of basic Digital Publicity or use of some promotional articles.
- 25% of the populations present the existence of an inventory of tourist attractions, although without a formal structure.

Table 3. Characteristics of the Magic Peoples in involvement phase.

Region	Locality	Year of incorporation	Characteristics
North	Batopilas, Chihuahua	2012	-Positive and slow national and foreigners' arrivals. -Nature resources conservation. -Big number of tourist periods during the year. -Limited terrestrial and air connectivity. -Few tourist services basic and offered by the local population. -Publicity in Internet. -Regulated urban image.
	El Rosario, Sinaloa	2012	-Positive but slow arrivals. -Limited number of tourist periods. -Tourist attractions of cultural type. -Limited connectivity. -Rendering of tourist service for the residents. -Incipient publicity. -Regulated urban image.
Gulf of Mexico	Mier, Tamaulipas	2007	-Inventory of tourist attractions exists with small offer. -Conservation comes up of tourist resources. -Small offer of tourist services. -Few connectivity. -There is no information on tourist employment. -There does not exist publicity that generates an attractive image of the place.
	Tapijulapa, Tabasco	2010	-Arrivals of positive but slow visitors. -They predominate over activities and natural tourist attractions, on activities and resources of cultural type. -Good connectivity terrestrial but lacking in suitable signalling. -Small, local and scarce tourist structure. -Limited contribution of the tourism to the local economic development.
	Xico, Veracruz	2011	-Arrivals of national visitors. -It exist inventory of tourist attractions. -Conservation comes up of the attractions. -Limited connectivity to the place. -Limited offer of tourist services. -Limited tourist employment. -Good index of satisfaction of the user. -Perceptible changes in the physical appearance of the place. -Incipient digital publicity.
Pacific Ocean	Tlalpujahua, Michoacán	2005	-Positive but slow visits. -Good facilities in attractions, but their limited quantity. -Perceptible changes in the area. -Average publicity and connectivity and in growth. -There is information neither on satisfaction of the visitor, nor on tourist employment. -Local sufficiency in the offer of tourist services.
	Capulálpam, Oaxaca	2007	-Limited number of tourist periods, but with visitor´s inflow. -Quite preserved attractive natives exist. -Incipient connectivity. -Limited offer of tourist services. -Good public safety. -Environmental practices -Employment is generated little in the sector. -Scope publicity does not exist.
	San Sebastián del Oeste, Jalisco	2011	-Continuous visitors arrivals but reduced. -The summer is identified like the tourist period. -Major number of cultural attractions. -There does not exist information about the tourist activity in the local development. -Sufficient offer of basic tourist services. -Limited connectivity for the access to the place. -Limited digital publicity.
	Jala, Nayarit	2012	-Limited number of tourist periods. -Positive but slow arrivals. -Sufficiency of attractions tourist, but lacking in activities. -Almost void offer of basic tourist services. -Limited terrestrial connectivity. -Information does not exist on tourist employment. -Publicity in Internet. -Urban rules do not exist.

(Continued)

Table 3. (Continued).

Region	Locality	Year of incorporation	Characteristics
Central	Real de Asientos, Aguascalientes	2006	-Tourists' fair amount only in Holy Week and summer. -There is no resources inventory. -Good grade of conservation of attractions. -The attractions are commercialized specially and are provided with facilities. -Perceptible changes in the local physical appearance. -tourist employment begins to be generated. -Very limited offer of tourist services. -Incipient connectivity.
	Jerez, Zacatecas	2007	-Enough terrestrial connectivity exists. -Limited number of tourist periods. -Plenty of resources of cultural type, but without tourist use by means of activities. -Insufficient promotion. -Limited offer of services tourist and lacking in quality. -There are no programmes of urban progress. -Little public safety. -Practices of sustainability do not exist.
	Metepec, Estado de México	2012	-Visitors and tourists of very short demurrage. -Limited offer of tourist resources. -Sufficient offer of tourist services of feeding and transport. -Quality in the public service rendering. -Good connectivity to the destination. -Tourist periods are not identified. -Regulated urban image. -Internet portals.
	Salvatierra, Guanajuato	2012	-Local and regional visitors. -Sufficient offer of tourist attractions. -Terrestrial connectivity exists. -Quality in the public service rendering. -Small offer of basic tourist services. -There is no scope publicity. -The tourism generates little employment.
	Yuriria, Guanajuato	2012	-There exists inflow of national visitors and few foreigners. -Sufficient offer of cultural and natural attractions. -Limited terrestrial connectivity. -There is no scope publicity. -Limited offer of basic tourist services. -The tourism generates little employment. -There are no rules for urban image.
	Nochistlán, Zacatecas	2012	-Limited number of tourist periods. -Positive visitors arrivals but very slow. -Sufficiency in resources of natural type. Few cultural attractions in the average conservation state. -There is no active use of the tourist resources. -Only terrestrial connectivity exists, but it is good. -Good public service rendering. -Scarce offer of tourist services and of bad quality. -Perceptible changes in the local physical appearance. -Practically void promotion of the destination.
South	Palizada, Campeche	2010	-Positive visitor's arrivals. -A tourist period of the destination is not identified clearly. -Existence of an inventory of tourist resources. -Limited offer of tourist services. -The tourism begins to be an option that he contributes to the local development. -Magic Village does not identify the value of the mark for the locality. -Engagement equality does not exist in the performance of community and of authorities.

Source: Table compiled based on Ministry of Tourism (2014b).

- Some attractions have begun to be provided with good facilities in 25% of the localities in involvement.
- In 43.75%, perceptible changes are identified in the urban image of the localities.
- In 31.25% of these territories, there exist negotiations that allow the conservation of attractions of natural type by means of the implementation and execution of environmental practices.

Once stated the main results of the investigations, we present the conclusions in the following section.

Conclusion and implications

The Diagnoses of Competitiveness and Tourist Sustainability of the Magic Peoples contributed valuable information that allowed, to delimit with major wise move, the characteristics of the localities of the sample and determine with objectivity its life trajectory in the field of the tourism. This facilitated the achievement of the intention of this study, which was to identify to localities inscribed in the Magic Peoples Program of Mexico that are in the involvement phase in its life cycle and the elements that characterize this stage, as well as others that begin giving direction towards a later phase. Certainly, the biggest number of the populations catalogued in this phase becomes attached to the characteristics of the model proposed by Butler (1980), but the results reveal that the proper elements of this stage are still not consolidated appropriately and, in turn, they are fused by the effort towards other components that are typical of the following stage in the model of life cycle that served like study frame.

Although it is suitable to deal with aspects that delimit advance in a pre-existence process, it is profitable to strengthen first the initial steps with specific actions and later to continue with subsequent actions that should lead to another phase, but on the base of tasks and quite definite results. In this sense, the obtained common finds for the localities Magic Peoples in involvement phase, bear consequently, to the achievement of valuable negotiations that help to improve the conditions detected across this study, such as identifying seasonal periods based on their offer and demand, systematize the obtaining of relevant information for planning and effective decision-making, the structural and functional assess-ment of cultural attractions, to programme them, creative activities that generate an interesting tourist experience for visitors and promote the creation of local companies for the supply of basic tourist services.

The findings also revealed the existence of actions with which the localities have initiated an advance towards the stage of development in their life cycle, which imply focusing on such aspects like to promote the joint work of community and government, specify actions on construction of infrastructure, planning of tourist attractions, strategies of promotion and commercialization of the destination, implementation of good environmental practices and the creation of programmes of public safety. With these actions, one will help to grant a competitive position to every Magic Village and, at the same time, it will be possible to guarantee its permanence inside the Magic Peoples Program of Mexico. But it is also important to point out that tourism managers must realize that the actions that are carried out require defined strategies based on models of tourism competitiveness that allow to consolidate the achievements obtained by these populations in their involvement phase and also enable them to give step to growth and progress in its life cycle within the tourism sector.

Disclosure statement

No potential conflict of interest was reported by the authors.

ORCID

Juan Ignacio Pulido-Fernández ⓘ http://orcid.org/0000-0002-9019-726X

References

Agarwal, S. (2002). Restructuring seaside tourism: The resort life cycle. *Annals of Tourism Research, 29*(1), 25–55.

Buhalis, D. (2000). Marketing the competitive destination of the future. *Tourism Management, 21*, 97–116.

Butler, R. (1980). The concept of a tourist area cycle of evolution: Implications for management of resources. *The Canadian Geographer, 24*, 5–12.

Choy, D. (1992). Life cycle models for Pacific Island destinations. *Journal of Travel Research, 30*(3), 26–31.

Cooper, C., & Jackson, S. (1989). Destination life cycle: The Isle of Man case study. *Annals of Tourism Research, 16*, 377–398.

Digance, J. (1997). Life cycle model. *Research Notes and Reports, 24*, 452–456.

France, L. (1991). An application of the tourism destination area life cycle to Barbados. *The Tourist Review, 2*, 25–31.

Garay, L., & Cànoves, G. (2011). Life cycles, stages and tourism history: The Catalonia (Spain) experience. *Annals of Tourism Research, 38*(2), 651–671.

García, B., Reinares, E., & Armelini, G. (2013). Ciclo de vida de los destinos turísticos y estrategias de comunicación: Los casos de España y Chile [Destination life cycle and communication strategies: Cases of Spain and Chile]. *Revista Internacional de Investigación en Comunicación aDResearch ESIC, 7*(7), 76–93.

García, J. (2011). Cuenca: Un destino turístico consolidado [Cuenca, Spain – A consolidated tourism destination]. *Cuadernos de Turismo, 27*, 403–418.

Gonçalves-Gândara, J. M., Domareski, T., Chim, A., & Biz, A. (2013). El ciclo de vida y el posicionamiento competitivo de los productos turísticos de Foz de Iguaçu desde la perspectiva de los actores locales [Destination life cycle and competitive positioning of tourism products in Foz de Iguaçu from residents´ perspective]. *Investigaciones Turísticas, 6*, 1–26.

González, R. C., & Mendieta, M. D. (2009). Reflexiones sobre la Conceptualización de la Competitividad de Destinos Turísticos [Reflections to conceptualise tourism destination comopetitiveness]. *Cuadernos de Turismo, 23*, 111–128.

Hovinen, G. (2002). Revisiting the destination life cycle model. *Annals of Tourism Research, 29*(1), 209–230.

Jiménez, P., & Aquino, F. K. (2012). Propuesta de un modelo de competitividad de destinos turísticos [Proposal of a model for tourism competitiveness]. *Estudios y Perspectivas en Turismo, 21*(4), 977–995.

Ministry of Tourism. (2014a). *Acuerdo por el que se establecen los Lineamientos Generales para la incorporación y permanencia al Programa Pueblos Mágicos* [Agreement for developing the Projct of Pueblos Mágicos]. México: Secretaría de Turismo. Diario Oficial de la Federación.

Ministry of Tourism. (2014b). *Diagnósticos de Competitividad y Sustentabilidad de los Pueblos Mágicos* [Diagnosis for competivieness and sustainability of Pueblos Mágicos]. México: Secretaría de Turismo. Retrieved from https://www.gob.mx/sectur/acciones-y-programas/programa-pueblos-magicos

Montaño, A., Pérez, J. C., & De la O, V. (2014). Reposicionamiento para destinos turísticos consolidados: El caso de Los Cabos, México [Repositioning tourism destinations: Case of Los Cabos, Mexico]. *Cuadernos de Turismo, 33*, 271–295.

Ngaire, D. (1997). Applying the life cycle model to Melanesia. *Annals of Tourism Research, 24*(1), 1–22.

Oreja, J. R., Parra, E., & Yanes, V. (2008). The sustainability of island destination: Tourism area life cycle and teleological perspectives, the case of Tenerife. *Tourism Management, 29,* 53–65.

Pérez, C., & Páez, A. I. (2014). El turismo de eventos y reuniones en destinos turísticos maduros: Un pilar para la reconversión del producto turístico de Puerto de la Cruz (Tenerife) [Event and meetings' tourism in mature destinations: Case of Puerto de la Cruz, Tenerife, Spain]. *Investigaciones Turísticas, 7,* 102–135.

Pike, S. (2009). Destination brand positions of a competitive set of near-home destinations. *Tourism Management, 30,* 857–866.

Ritchie, J. R. B., & Crouch, G. I. (2000). The competitive destination: A sustainability perspective. *Tourism Management, 21,* 1–7.

Ritchie, J. R. B., & Crouch, G. I. (2003). *The competitive destination: A sustainable tourism perspective.* Wallingford: CAB International Publishing.

Schuckert, M., Möller, C., & Weiermair, K. (2007). Alpine destination life cycles: Challenges and implications. *Trends and Issues in Global Tourism, 2007,* 121–136.

Soares, J., Gândara, J., & Ivars, J. (2012). Indicadores para analizar la evolución del ciclo de vida de los destinos turísticos litorales [Indicators for the analysis of life cycle in seaside tourism destinations]. *Investigaciones Turísticas, 3,* 19–38.

Vera, J. F., & Baños, C. J. (2010). Renovación y reestructuración de los destinos turísticos consolidados del litoral: Las prácticas recreativas en la evolución del espacio turístico [Renovating and restructuring of tourism seaside destinations]. *Boletín de la Asociación de Geógrafos Españoles, 53,* 329–353.

Virgen, C. R. (2009). El ciclo de vida de un destino turístico: Puerto Vallarta, Jalisco, México [Life cycle of a tourism destination: Case of Puerto Vallarta, Jalisco, México]. *CULTUR-Revista de Cultura e Turismo, 1,* 1–24.

Border medical tourism: the Ciudad Juárez medical product

Maria Teresa Martínez Almanza, Jaume Guía Julve, Santos Alonso Morales Muñoz
and María Angélica Esparza Santillana

ABSTRACT
The pursuit of cross-border health care between the United States and
Mexico has been a common practice for decades. Patients in the United
States are motivated to seek medical attention in Ciudad Juárez, Mexico, due
to several factors: affordability of treatment abroad, access to treatments not
available at home, considerable cost differentiation, as well as long waiting
lists to receive medical attention at home, among others. The results of 28
interviews with the main stakeholders are presented in this article, with the
purpose of achieving a better understanding of border medical tourism. The
results show a medical tourism product differentiated by various health care
needs and the income of patients.

Introduction

In the process of tourism development, one of the most important challenges for people and
companies is the creation of new tourism products, which are expected to be novel, relevant and
profitable for both supply and demand (Barbosa, 2007). Medical tourism is a distinct market niche
in the tourism industry (Connell, 2006), and has grown rapidly to become an international
economic sector where people travel to other countries to obtain medical, dental and surgical
care, while at the same time enjoy a holiday period (Heung, Kucukusta, & Song, 2010). The main
cause of this growth is the difference in the cost of treatments, other relevant reasons being long
waiting lists and treatments not available at home.

On the United States-Mexico border, the health industry is expanding rapidly due to the
growth of their private sector and especially the presence of medical tourism, which has emerged
as a lucrative business opportunity. Health services in Ciudad Juárez sought by patients crossing
the Juárez-El Paso border are the focus of this article, which aims to achieve a better understanding of medical tourism and its operation at the borders, and which medical services are more
frequently requested in the case analyzed. Therefore, the following research question is posed:
how is the medical tourism product characterized in a border city?

To answer the research question, a case clearly representative of the phenomenon under study
has been chosen: Ciudad Juárez, Chihuahua, Mexico, bordering El Paso, Texas in the United
States, after several decades of development of medical tourism in an international border context.

The authors reviewed a wide range of bibliographic resources and analyzed data obtained
through 28 in-depth interviews. The main interviewed participants included: personnel from
private hospitals, governmental agencies, civil society organizations, institutions and physicians.

The interview data were analyzed thematically using deductive and inductive codes that captured key concepts through the narratives of the participants.

Many studies examining the phenomena of medical tourism from the patient's perspective, have identified characteristics of the most demanded products associated with this global health services practice (De la Puente, 2015; Ormond & Sothern, 2012; Regis, Epps, & Bernier, 2013), however, there is a lack of attention of medical care and services, provided by doctors, at the border cities in existing research. To date, researchers have not sufficiently examined the types of medical tourism product on borders. In this article, we fill this gap by examining the product of medical tourism and the characteristics of the medical product and complementary services. Therefore, this research contributes to the study of medical tourism in a border city to academic literature as that the modus operandi of a medical tourism destination located at the border has not yet been sufficiently studied (Horton & Cole, 2011).

Some companies that are dedicated to facilitate these trips, focus more on providing quick access to medical procedures, than combining medical care with vacations, as in the case of the border of Ciudad Juárez Chihuahua, Mexico with El Paso, Texas and Las Cruces, New Mexico, in the United States (Martínez-Almanza, Julve Guía, & Serra Salame, 2014).

The article is divided into four sections. First, a literature review is presented highlighting the importance of the medical tourism product; the second part refers to the analytical process of preparing the manuscript; then the results of the investigation are shown, and finally, the conclusions and implications are offered.

Literature review

The tourist product has been studied by Connell (2006) and Yu and Ko (2012) who reports that "in some destinations, including Hungary and the Republic of Mauritius, the possibilities of medical tourism are announced in the flight magazines and in the government's tourism publications, on the assumption that tourists can resort to small-scale medical procedures such as dentistry during conventional tourist visits" (p. 1098). Even when medical treatment is the main product, attractive hospitality and good travel options are also essential. Therefore, a medical tourism product is a health product with an attractive component for leisure time (Heung et al., 2010).

The study of borders and medical tourism has been mentioned as an issue in which there is a need to deepen the understanding. Connell (2013) states that "Medical tourism is now seen as a relatively short, transboundary and diasporic distance" (p. 1), and also asserts that it is of limited severity despite the aesthetic surgery that dominates the media debates.

The segmentation of the medical tourism market is a topic that has been studied by Caballero and Mugomba (2006) and Wendt (2012). Goodrich and Goodrich (1987), pioneers in the study of this type of tourism, affirm that in health tourism there are at least two possible forms of market segmentation: health and income. On the other hand, Alsharif, Labonté, and Lu (2010) state that the cost of services, the reputation of the doctor and accreditation are the most important factors when choosing health care abroad. Gan and James (2011) have studied the nature of market differentiation of medical tourism facilitators in the United States, and they express that it resembles an industry of monopolistic competition. They choose to differentiate services in several ways, including the list of countries and hospitals medical tourists use, the scope of the treatments they specialize in, the degree of participation of medical professionals in the company, and the types of auxiliary services that they offer.

Ormond (2014) affirms that migrant diasporas are increasingly linked as "natural" markets and "ambassadors" to the world-class private health care progressively available in their countries of origin. Rerkrujipimol and Assenov (2011) evaluate current marketing strategies of medical tourism providers and intermediaries in Thailand. The above-mentioned works refer to the overseas medical tourism. This research differs from most studies of this phenomenon, since it refers to this activity with the particularities of cross-border mobility that occurs in border cities.

Methodology

The selected methodological approach was exploratory. "Medical tourism is a new area that has not yet been fully explored" (Heung, Kucukusta, & Song, 2011, p. 998). Being a novel phenomenon, within the scope of application, it requires a framework that provides flexibility to be able to inquire about the topic. Following the ideas of Selltiz, Jahoda, Deutsch, and Cook (1965), this study provides a flexible framework that allows achieving a more precise understanding of the phenomenon in order to generate an empirical basis for the research.

The methodology used in this article falls within the qualitative approach. The basic method selected was grounded theory (Glaser & Strauss, 1967), which refers essentially to any type of research that produces findings not obtained through statistical procedures or quantification. This work seeks to gain an understanding of human actions and to comprehend the reality of the phenomenon through an inductive process.

The selection of the approach and the techniques used was derived from the contextualization of the study area and the definition of research objectives. These elements favoured the inclination towards a qualitative approach, since they coincide with the ideas of Brewer and Hunter (1989) who mention the importance acquired by qualitative studies in the face of the difficulty of identifying a population, under study, in health-related subjects.

Selected stakeholders

Based on Caballero and Mugomba (2006) model, and Heung et al. (2010) who have studied the medical tourism stakeholders, the following categories of stakeholders were selected.

Primary information

The 28 in-depth interviews were conducted with an average length of 60 min. Authors started the process of interviewee selection in the four hospitals that Chihuahua's State Government, through which the Ministry of Economy started developing a cluster of medical tourism. Two of them belong to the most prestigious hospital chains in the country, so they offer quality services and scientific and technological progress in its health infrastructure. The other two institutions are the most recognized by the communities on both sides of the border. Two additional hospitals located very close to the international crossings at Juarez-El Paso were selected because of this proximity to the border. The process of obtaining primary information began with interviews with senior staff of these hospitals.

Sampling

A non-probabilistic sampling was used with a variety of criteria like expertise in the research topic, ability and willingness of the participants who would be more likely to provide adequate data, and others. This type of sampling known as "purposive sampling" has been used by several authors in studies of medical tourism (Crooks et al., 2012; Hunter-Jones, 2005; Rerkrujipimol & Assenov, 2011). The technique of "snowball" was afterwards used to obtain from participants their recommendation of other actors who had relevant experience, knowledge and ability to collaborate in interviews. This technique was chosen because of the positive assessment of its use in identifying "best informants (Casey, Crooks, Snyder, & Turner, 2013; Crooks et al., 2012; Glinos, Baeten, Helble, & Maarse, 2010; Glinos et al., 2010; Hanefeld, Lunt, Smith, & Horsfall, 2014; Snyder, Crooks, & Johnston, 2012).

Data analysis

A qualitative study by Casey et al. (2013) on the roles of informal caregivers of medical tourism patients was taken as reference for the method of analysis. The thematic analysis involved six steps: (i) reviewing the interviews' transcripts and notes; (ii) pooling: in a face to face meeting with the research group, findings on issues that were emerging and outliers were discussed; (iii) creating a preliminary coding scheme which identified the general thematic concepts and components; (iv) encoding the data in N-Vivo, with advice on refinement and interpretation by the group of research; (v) identification of trends and relevant patterns of the issues under analysis, namely those concerning medical tourism destination development, and the identification of important topics related to the medical tourism product; (vi) disclosing a more refined interpretation of the meaning in the encoded data through a comparative of trends and patterns with existing knowledge, which was exposed to the other researchers for confirmation. The review was concluded when new information was no longer obtained (Dunn, 1986; Patton, 1990).

Axial coding allowed grouping the refined subcategories to identify the main categories or themes (Dey, 1998; Strauss & Corbin, 2002) and the relationships between the topics to be identified. During this process, the themes and the main categories identified were validated by comparing the information provided by the different people interviewed and then comparing the information obtained in the interviews with the data obtained through the observation and analysis of secondary data. Finally, a framework was developed after reviewing the codified and categorized statements and the interrelationships between them were identified.

This analytical process allowed for the common themes to emerge despite differences in the type of medical tourism the participants engaged in, their work environment and work histories.

Results

By identifying the types of health services offered to medical tourism patients in Ciudad Juarez, a wide range of services available in different types of establishments was found, such as medical and dental offices, pharmacies, opticians, study cabinets and laboratories for cross-border population. Most of these service providers are located in areas near international crossings and they offer instant attention at a cost that brings important savings to patients. Additionally, it was found the existence of more economical or budget hospitals with proximity to international crossings, which operate within the medical tourism industry. There are hospitals that offer health care addressed to a population with low income, and provide basic specialties such as surgery, internal medicine and gynaecology.

The medical tourism product of greater demand on the border of Juarez-El Paso has traditionally been dentistry services, which includes general dentistry, such as fillings and extractions, as well as specialized dentistry, which offers oral rehabilitation care and implantology (see Table 1). However, in the last decade there has been a significant increase in the medical services requested by cross-border visitors, including ophthalmology, bariatric surgery and cosmetic surgery, as well as consultations with health specialists in different areas of specialty, such as orthopaedics, cardiology, dermatology, gynaecology, among others.

Table 1. Main actors by group of stakeholders categories.

Categories of stakeholders	Interviews carried out
Government Sector	4
Hospitals	6
Specialist Doctors	7
Tourism Sector	5
Social Groupings	3
Education Sector	3
Total	28

Table 2. Supply of health services in Ciudad Juárez. Establishments located in streets close to international bridges.

Zone/Bridge	Dentists	Phamacies	Doctors	Opticians	Laboratory and X-Rays	Clínics	Hospitals	Total	%
The Americas	35	10	13	5	6	2	2	73	55
Santa Fe	7	5	1	8	1	0	1	23	17
Zaragoza	17	7	5	7	0	0	1	37	28
Totals	59	22	19	20	7	2	4	133	100

Table 2 shows that more than half of the identified health businesses are located near the Americas Bridge (near the border). In addition, there are two hospitals and state-of-the-art facilities, in locations 20 min from the international bridges that offer more complex, high-quality, and high-cost hospitalization activities and specialties such as cardiac surgery, neurosurgery, and transplants.

The existence of dental and ophthalmological services was also noted. Some clinics and dental offices are highly specialized and use the most advanced technology and materials, with a better aesthetic image of their facilities and infrastructure. They are located in avenues that offer a better image of the city and their health specialists have prestigious professional trajectories and recognitions for the quality of their services.

Who are the "tourists" who seek cross-border health care?

In the framework outlined above and based on the problems faced by a large part of the population of the United States and Canada, it was identified that patients seeking health care at the border is a very diverse group, which can be classified according to their income and their health (Goodrich & Goodrich, 1987).

In terms of income

There are patients who seek medical care at a lower cost. Hospitals with specialists, and surgeons, such as the Hospital de la Familia, which operates within a non-profit organization structure, receive around 36,000 patients from the diaspora annually. In the same way, there are those who only buy medicines at *Similares* pharmacies, which are advertised as "the leading pharmaceutical chain in sales and distribution in Mexico and Latin America, where you will find quality generics [drugs] at the best prices". Around 95% of the people who go to these types of hospitals and pharmacies are patients of limited purchasing power and of Mexican origin located in the neighbouring U.S. cities and towns on the border, such as El Paso, Canutillo, Clint, Tornillo, Chaparral, Horizon, Vinton, Odessa, and Midland, in the state of Texas, and Las Cruces and Anthony, in the State of New Mexico.

Most of the patients who currently cross the border to receive health care in Ciudad Juárez, do so to have consultation with medical specialists, since the cost of these service can be between 500 and 800 pesos, which is equivalent to an average of 25 to 40 USD. This contrasts with specialized medical consultation in the United States, which could cost around 250 USD, involving savings of more than 80%.

Also, the presence of Anglo patients seeking bariatric surgery services was identified. In these cases, the opposite happens in contrast with the previous case. They are patients that afford to pay for a stay in luxury hospitals. The price of a bariatric surgery, on average is 10,000.00 USD in Mexico, while in the United States it could cost 30,000.00–35,000.00 USD, which represents an estimated saving of 65%. It should be mentioned that this service is not found in the catalogue of coverage of medical insurance in the United States and patients have to pay out of pocket. The interviewed bariatric specialist reported conducting an average of 60–65 surgeries per month.

In terms of health problems

The majority of patients who currently cross the border to receive health care in Ciudad Juárez do so in order to receive consultation from medical specialists. The subjects interviewed mentioned that 80% of the patients who come to a medical consultation seek treatment for chronic diseases.

With regard to the age of the visitors, a cardiovascular surgeon mentioned that his patients' age range is from 40 to 65 years old.

> *The people who come to Ciudad Juárez, to this hospital, seek medical attention, that is, medical consultation; they also spend on other things, but it is not international tourism where people travel due to major problems or surgeries. Here they come for consultation. Eventually, they look for surgeries, but really the bulk of the patients, come for a medical consultation.*

The services with greatest demand are usually those not covered by health insurance, such as dentistry and bariatric surgery, which have a strong presence in the medical tourism sector in the city.

Conclusion and implications

In the segmentation of the market at least two criteria have been observed: (i) health and (ii) people's income. They were linked to geographical, demographic, psychographic, price, use and benefits' aspects. Below are some concomitant conclusions on these aspects.

Geographical aspects: proximity to the market of the United States gives the border destination a significant competitive advantage for the development of medical tourism. It reduces the risks involved in not having to travel many hours with the respective health implications and costs for the patients.

Demographic aspects: there is a great potential for medical tourism development, since a third of the U.S. population, over 300 million people, lack health coverage in the United States; in addition, the ageing of the baby boom population is a factor that will exert a significant pressure on the demand for health services and where chronic diseases such as obesity and cardiovascular diseases are a serious problem. Also, the specialized dentistry service is one of the most representative services that has existed for several decades in the city and continues to be an important point of attraction for cross-border patients.

This is the main health segment for medical tourism in Ciudad Juarez. Therefore, in neighbouring countries where there is an important diaspora, as in the case of Mexico and the United States, where there are more than twenty million Mexicans, this population becomes a natural market that could be sought to be served at the border if the desirable conditions of services are provided. It is also important to mention that the barrier of language and cultural distance is diluted in these cases.

Psychographic aspects: the familiarity with border crossing of the diaspora visitors is an advantage that can be related to the personality and tastes of diaspora patients. This aspect, which involves border customs procedures, can be intimidating for international patients.

Prices of services' aspects: it is concluded that price is one of the most important factors in attracting international patients with health problems, whose income is not sufficient to cover their medical expenses in their country of residence.

Use and benefits' aspects: there is a considerable growth in the demand of patients mainly from the diaspora who are seeking the benefit of satisfying their needs for consultation with medical specialists and to a lesser degree, with surgeons. These patients recommend the services acquired to their family and friends and this is the main way of promoting cross-border health services' consumption. These types of results in border tourism differ from those in the literature, where online marketing is given a predominant place for the success of the medical destination.

This study thus contributes to the construction of the understanding of medical tourism, its development process, and the way of operation of this industry in border areas. The results obtained in the case of Ciudad Juárez – El Paso border could be similar in other border regions where there is a diaspora with a strong sense of nation, that is, with values, ideology, cultural identity, and interests related to their country of origin.

It has also been found that, in addition to dental services, which are the most requested, the four other main services are oncology, ophthalmology, plastic surgery and bariatric surgery.

However, the demand for the treatment of health problems, which is addressed by providers of health care services in Ciudad Juarez, allows for the identification of a differentiated destination health product. The medical destination has been developing for several decades a diverse range of health services to which patients who seek services at the border have responded favourably. This differentiation consists of creating a range of services for different market segments. Thus, there are hospitals and clinics strategically located in proximity to international crossings and patients where they find medical attention for different needs of treatment and prices in both, budget hospital and clinics, as well as luxury medical facilities.

Another element that favours the satisfaction of the patients is the warm treatment they receive from health professionals, which is an element of emotional satisfaction that influences loyalty to the destination (Kotler, 2000). This author mentions the importance of creating more satisfactory solutions to the needs of consumers. Although, he does not refer to emotional aspects, but cognitive or rational ones, there is the need of further knowledge about the emotional aspects of the satisfaction of patients-consumers of medical tourism. Loyalty is important because customers provide recommendations, positive reviews, and the best advertising, which affects increased revenue. The benefits of loyalty to the most traditional doctors and hospitals of the city are clearly observed.

Regarding innovation, hospitals and dental clinics have implemented safe transportation to take patients from El Paso to Ciudad Juárez to be treated and take them back to their homes or to the airport if required.

It is concluded that the suppliers of health services are reaching a large and diverse number of individuals. This is due to consumer patients belonging to distinct market segments. Therefore, the destination offers a well-differentiated product, perhaps as the result of an emergent, unplanned process, rather than as the outcome of an active policy and an effective strategy.

The results of this research contribute to the literature by revealing the characteristics of medical tourism in border areas. They are also valuable for practitioners in Mexico and other countries willing to develop this industry. Results also show the existence of different types of medical tourism, which have not yet been sufficiently studied in the literature, particularly the aspect of frontier territory, which adds elements that have not yet been considered in depth analysis of the issue, or aspects of marketing in these scenarios.

The analysis of the demand side is necessary to highlight the key points of what medical tourists expect to find in a border destination and how to attract them. The results of the study also have implications for the quality of medical and hospitality services in a single institution and for the industry at large. Studies of the supply side provide valuable information on medical tourism institutions in terms of promotional activities and infrastructure and superstructure development. It is necessary to analyze and compare the demand and supply factors in a given country or region, as well as their interactions with the decisions made by medical tourists, as they will reveal the managerial and structural approaches taken by all of the market players in the medical tourism industry.

Acknowledgements

We would like to thank all the health and tourism representatives from Ciudad Juárez, who gave their time to participate in this study. This research was funded by a "Programa de Mejoramiento del Profesorado" (Professors Improvement Program) Grant, from the Secretaría de Educación Pública from Mexico's Federal government.

Disclosure statement

No potential conflict of interest was reported by the authors.

References

Alsharif, M. J., Labonté, R., & Lu, Z. (2010). Patients beyond borders: A study of medical tourists in four countries. *Global Social Policy, 10*(3), 315–335.

Barbosa, M. (2007). The policy of cultural tourism and tourism product design for cultural tourism. Case: Tourist corridor Bogota Boyacá-Santander. *EAN Magazine*, (60), 105–122.

Brewer, J., & Hunter, A. (1989). *Multimethod research: A synthesis of styles.* Newbury Park, California: Sage.

Caballero, S., & Mugomba, C. (2006). *Medical Tourism and Its Entrepreneurial opportunities. A conceptual framework for entry into the industry.*

Casey, V., Crooks, V. A., Snyder, J., & Turner, L. (2013). Knowledge brokers, companions, and navigators: A qualitative examination of the informal caregivers' roles in medical tourism. *International Journal for Equity in Health, 12*(94). doi:10.1186/1475-9276-12-94

Connell, J. (2006). Medical tourism: Sea, sun, sand and … surgery. *Tourism Management, 27*(6), 1093–1100.

Connell, J. (2013). Contemporary medical tourism: Conceptualization, culture and commodification. *Tourism Management, 34*, 1–13.

Crooks, V., Cameron, K., Chouinard, V., Johnston, R., Snyder, J., & Casey, V. (2012). Use of medical tourism for hip and knee surgery in osteoarthritis: A qualitative examination of distinctive attitudinal Characteristics among Canadian patients. *BMC Health Services, 12*(1), 417.

De la Puente, M. (2015). Sector del Turismo de Salud: Caso de Colombia [Health Tourism Sector: Case of Colombia]. *Caribbean Economy Magazine[Revista De Economía Del Caribe]*, (16), 129–161.

Dey, I. (1998). *Qualitative data analysis: A user friendly guide for social scientists.* London: Routledge.

Dunn, W. N. (1986). *Policy analysis: Perspectives, concepts, and methods.* Greenwich, CT: JAI Press.

Gan, L. L., & James, F. (2011). Medical tourism facilitators: Patterns of service differentiation. *Journal of Vacation Marketing, 17*(3), 165–183.

Glaser, B., & Strauss, A. (1967). The discovery of grounded theory. *International Journal of Qualitative Methods*, vol. 5. Retrieved from http://www.ualberta.ca/~iiqm/backissues/5_1/pdf/mills.pdf

Glinos, I., Baeten, R., Helble, M., & Maarse, H. (2010). A typology of cross-border patient mobility. *Health & Place, 16*, 1145–1155.

Goodrich, J., & Goodrich, G. (1987). Health-care tourism – An exploratory study. *Tourism Management*, 217–222. doi:10.1016/0261-5177(87)90053-7

Hanefeld, J., Lunt, N., Smith, R., & Horsfall, D. (2014). Why do medical tourists travel to where they do? The role of networks in determining medical travel. *Social Science & Medicine, 124*, 356–363.

Heung, V., Kucukusta, D., & Song, H. (2010). A conceptual model of medical tourism: Implications for future research. *Journal of Travel & Tourism Marketing, 27*(3), 236–251.

Heung, V., Kucukusta, D., & Song, H. (2011). Medical tourism development in Hong Kong: An assessment of the barriers. *Tourism Management, 32*, 995–1005.

Horton, S., & Cole, S. (2011). Medical returns: Seeking health care in Mexico. *Social Science & Medicine, 72*, 1846–1852.

Hunter-Jones, P. (2005). Cancer and Tourism. *Annals of Tourism Research, 32*(1), 70–92.

Kotler, P. (2000). *Marketing Management.* Upper Saddle River, New Jersey: Prentice Hall.

Martínez-Almanza, M. T., Julve Guía, J., & Serra Salame, C. (2014). Genesis and evolution of medical tourism. In *Tourism trends in Latin America.* Ciudad Juarez, Chihuahua, Mexico.

Ormond, M. (2014). Harnessing "diasporic" medical mobilities. In F. Thomas & J. Gideon (Eds.)*Migration, health and inequality* (pp. 150–162). London: Zed Books.

Ormond, M., & Sothern, M. (2012). You, too, can be an international medical traveler: Reading medical travel guidebooks. *Health & Place, 18*(5), 935–941.

Patton, M. (1990). *Qualitative evaluation and research methods.* Newbury Park, CA: Sage.

Regis, C., Epps, T., & Bernier, L. (2013). Implementing medical travel in the Canadian healthcare system: Considerations for policy makers - ProQuest. *Health Law Journal,* vol. *20.* Retrieved from http://search.proquest.com/docview/1467739986/fulltextPDF/22C81E651694402PQ/20?accountid=15295

Rerkrujipimol, J., & Assenov, I. (2011). Marketing strategies for promoting medical tourism in Thailand. *Journal of Tourism, Hospitality & Culinary Arts, 3*(2), 95–105.

Selltiz, C., Jahoda, M., Deutsch, M., & Cook, S. (1965). *Research methods in social relations.* Madrid: Holt, Rinehart and Winston.

Snyder, J., Crooks, V., & Johnston, R. (2012). Perceptions of the ethics of medical tourism: Comparing patient and academic perspectives. *Public Health Ethics, 5*(1), 38–46.

Strauss, A. L., & Corbin, J. 2002. *Basis of qualitative research: Techniques and procedures for developing grounded theory.* Medellín: University of Antioquia. Retrieved from http://cataleg.udg.edu/record=b1203227~S10*cat

Wendt, K. (2012). *Medical tourism: Trends and opportunities.* Las Vegas: University of Nevada.

Yu, J. Y., & Ko, T. G. (2012). A cross-cultural study of perceptions of medical tourism among Chinese, Japanese and Korean tourists in Korea. *Tourism Management, 33*(1), 80–88.

Competitiveness and innovation: effects on prosperity

Antonio García-Sánchez, David Siles and María de Mar Vázquez-Méndez

ABSTRACT
Competitiveness is a broad concept applied to many fields, especially economics. The study of tourism competitiveness has focused on factors that can enhance the prosperity of a destination. One of these factors is innovation. Innovation makes a destination's enterprises more advanced and efficient, therefore, more productive. The first studies about innovation in technology, consider it an incipient concept based only on activities such as internet use, but it has evolved into a wider concept changing the way of doing business. Innovation is not only an enhancer of competitiveness, it is a more relevant concept; it can be a generator of prosperity on its own because innovation in every aspect will provide a better quality of life for the destination.

Introduction

Competitiveness is a concept that applies to many aspects and enterprises. The capacity of companies to sell their products and obtain revenues is what makes them competitive (Porter, 1990). Competitiveness was later applied to fields like tourism. Tourism is a growing industry around the world, and most countries offer tourism experiences with the objective of earning revenues to improve their quality of life. These destinations must be competitive if they want to maintain or increase their tourism share.

The characteristics of a destination that attract visitors, earn revenue, satisfy tourists, and result in the final objective of prosperity (Crouch & Ritchie, 1999) is a definition of tourism competitiveness.

Some models try to define tourism competitiveness, and all of those models present competitiveness as a multidimensional concept. Several aspects of competitiveness can be measured through indicators. These models can help a destination be more competitive, so the search for a suitable group of indicators for any destination is a worthwhile task for researchers. The indicators are usually gathered in main categories, such as natural resources, location advantages, cultural legacy, tourism policy, and other important concepts regarding the destination's identity.

A competitive destination must be a place with a good quality of life where the inhabitants receive the benefits from tourism. When tourists visit the destination, they must feel that it is aesthetically pleasing and features plenty of resources that enrich their tourism experience. Sustainability is an essential element for a prosperous destination; therefore, competitiveness focuses on ensuring prosperity.

The variables that increase the competitiveness of a destination include those related to innovation, such as telecommunication systems, training programmes for employees, or use of technology. The effectiveness of innovation as an indicator of competitiveness is confirmed in the tourism competitiveness models. The integrated model (Dwyer & Kim, 2003) considers elements of innovation and technology in the determinants of competitiveness.

The way that innovation has become a relevant element in the business world creates implications at all levels. Innovative products and services are part of the destination's resources, and the inhabitants' way of life. People are in direct touch with new technologies for business and leisure. These changes spur contemplation about innovation as a concept that directly affects the socioeconomic prosperity of a destination.

The quality of life of a destination for the inhabitants and tourists will improve if innovation is developed. The innovative resources of a smart city can increase the comfort of tourists with amenities like Wi-Fi and electronic translators, as well as many advantages that increase sustainability such as improving the efficiency of energy resources.

Clearly, innovation can enhance the destination's competitiveness, increasing the effectiveness of the competitiveness indicators. Additionally, innovation offers a range of advantages that affect the quality of life of the destination. The capacity of innovation as a prosperity generator should be considered.

Literature review

Competitiveness is a concept present in many aspects of society and can be defined, generally, as the ability to sell products and receive benefits and resources (Scott & Lodge, 1985).

In this article, we focus on tourism competitiveness. Tourism is a relevant sector in many countries that contributes to the economy in a significant manner (Travel & Council, 2017). During the last century, many countries implemented polices focused on tourism (World Economic Forum, 2017).

The increase in the importance of tourism for economies has enhanced tourism competitiveness research. Tourism competitiveness can be defined as the capacity of a destination provide a certain quality of life to its inhabitants (Crouch & Ritchie, 1999). This concept is complex and comprises a range of indicators that may differ depending on the characteristics of each destination (Porter, Sachs, & McArthur, 2001); nevertheless, tourism competitiveness must be oriented to attain economic growth and prosperity.

An analysis of tourism competitiveness should be performed at the destinations to improve their performance and prosperity (Dwyer & Kim, 2003). The suitability of the indicators used to perform this analysis depend on the characteristics of the various destinations. The indicators must contain demand and supply indicators to ensure every aspect is considered (Kozak & Rimmington, 1999). Therefore, a more detailed study would be necessary to determine the most suitable indicators in every case.

One of the first and more complete models of tourism competitiveness is the 'integrated model' (Dwyer & Kim, 2003), in which a conceptual framework is established. The model defines the determinants of competitiveness that a destination must manage based on concepts such as resources, destination management, location conditions, and demand conditions.

Every group of competitiveness is measured by several indicators that define the concept. As Perna, Custódio, and Oliveira (2018) comment, destination management is the ability to manage and monitor these indicators and provides an additional advantage for tourism destination competitiveness.

Competitiveness and prosperity

Ritchie and Crouch (2003) present a more complete model that integrates features of demand. They define destination competitiveness, in general, as a destination's capacity to raise tourist expenditures and attract and satisfy visitors; additionally, this must be performed in a sustainable manner while achieving profit margins and positively affecting inhabitants' well-being.

The consequence of tourism destination competitiveness is prosperity. Buhalis (2000) talks about prosperity and defines competitiveness as work toward prosperity and achieving it in the long run. Dwyer and Kim (2003) state that competitiveness is a national issue, and the ultimate goal is to improve revenue and prosperity.

Other authors insist that quality of life is a sign of prosperity. Crouch and Ritchie (1999) assert that improvement in the competitiveness of a destination leads to an improvement in its inhabitants' quality of life, and destinations compete for mainly economic reasons. According to Dwyer, Livaic, and Mellor (2003), the ultimate aim of competitiveness must be to increase the destination's inhabitants' standard of living. This improvement can be achieved by increasing their revenue, "destination competitiveness is itself an intermediate goal towards a more fundamental aim of the economic wellbeing for residents". Similarly, Hong (2008) asserts that destination competitiveness increases revenue and quality of life through a destination's competitive position in the tourist industry.

Competitiveness is related to productivity. Newall (1992) comments that a competitive economy should be productive and sustainable for improving quality of life at destination. Wysokinska (2003) affirms that with productivity, costs can be reduced so prices will be lower, employment will increase, and the quality of life will be higher.

Porter, Sachs, and Warner (2000) conclude that a competitive economy leads to an increase in productivity and economic growth. Cadavid and Franco (2006) find a positive correlation between productivity and economic growth; thus, competitiveness is a key element in this relationship.

Regarding tourism destinations, Pulido and Sánchez-Rivero (2010) state that competitiveness and economic growth have a significative relation: an increase in tourism competitiveness produces an increase in tourism growth. Tourism's capacity to generate employment and expenses increases the destination's wellness and economic development.

Finally, we affirm that tourism destination competitiveness is related to socioeconomic prosperity and quality of life (Dwyer, Mellor, Livaic, Edwards, & Kim, 2004).

Innovation

When a product is improved or created, innovation occurs. Innovation could be defined as the development of an idea and its implementation in the markets (Bulc, 2011). That idea should provide a new product or service, or an improvement of the old one by adding new functions.

The business world has a high incidence of innovation. Companies search for innovations to their products to attain new customers or maintain their market share. The innovative advances in technology have provided an advanced industry that makes life and work easier. Innovation has played an important role in the advancement of industry (Freeman & Soete, 1997).

When innovating, different types of innovation can be performed: innovation of products or services, the production process, organization management and marketing, and human resources (Meneses & Teixeira, 2011).

The concept of product innovation is later transferred to the services field, where it has been applied to every aspect. A branch of the service industry where innovation is an important element for increasing competitiveness is tourism.

In tourism, innovation has affected information and communication technologies (ICT) significantly. Innovation has introduced new concepts that have changed working and formation methodology (Sancho & Maset, 1999). Tourism demand has evolved and is increasingly related with ICT; thus, adapting to demand on these terms is necessary.

Public organizations must encourage innovation with policies to support academic training and investment because with innovation, companies will earn more profits with fewer costs (Rosenberg, 2006). Then, companies' innovations should result in additional benefits. For example, in Spain, hotels with more innovations than their competitors attract more tourists; thus, these hotels are obtaining positive results and profits (Sundbo, Orfila-Sintes, & Sorensen, 2007).

Innovation and competitiveness

The literature is generally in agreement about how innovation is captured in tourism, relating it to tourism services and service processes, tourism-sector management (including human resources), marketing and diffusion, and the institutional component. Innovation aims to adapt current services or products to meet demand. Tourism demand has evolved and become more specialized; as such, destinations must innovate to attract new tourists, who are now accustomed to using ICT daily and seek new types of tourism and different experiences (Esteban, 2005).

Innovation is linked to competitiveness because innovation is necessary for maintaining competitiveness in an industry, and competitiveness is a requirement for maintaining or improving market standing. Innovation could entail using ICT for flights and cruises, making destinations more accessible and competitive because they attract more tourists. Cultural innovation could entail improvements to information access, such as smart cities; managing facilities; environmental sustainability; hotel human resource management; education programmes about the destination for the local inhabitants; and the marketing and promotion of travel, sport events, and other cultural factors. In summary, it is possible to innovate each innovation variable to increase productivity and, consequently, competitiveness (García-Sánchez & Siles, 2015b).

Notably, destinations that want to increase their competitiveness must innovate by improving one or more of the following: social media, management, technology, or service processes. Destination managers can identify where innovations are required and use our model as a guide for competing with other destinations.

Innovation provides a competitive advantage, resulting in profits and sustainable growth (Pavia, Stipanovic, & Mrnjavac, 2011). The search for innovation increases competitiveness and, as a direct effect, productivity, but with better products (Sundbo et al., 2007). As Sancho and Maset (1999) also affirm, innovation has a significative effect on productivity, and this effect increases competitiveness.

Specialization of a product, according to Porter (1990), spreads innovation. In Spain, the provinces with more specialized tourism contribute more; thus, they are more competitive (Sancho, 2008). Additionally, innovation is necessary to maintain the competitiveness position of the destinations. Buhalis (1998) indicates that destinations must use ICT and innovation methods in an organization to maintain their competitive position.

Innovation helps the destination increase competitiveness and the number of tourists. Victorino, Verma, Plaschaka, and Dev (2005) indicate that innovation garners competitive advantages and the customer's preference because destinations put efforts into attracting and satisfying a very sophisticated demand that looks for new experiences (Hu, Horng, & Sun, 2009). Innovation in the services available at the destination, particularly transport services, have been very important because it makes the distance between destinations feel shorter.

Innovation can reduce production costs; thus, it will increase productivity. Innovation is an essential condition in economic development, and a critical element in competitiveness (Freeman & Soete, 1997). Puccio and Grana (2008) also affirm that the innovation capacity of a destination is a relevant parameter in the destination competitiveness.

Innovation and prosperity

Hjalager (2010) comments that innovation in the tourism industry has provided benefits to managers and employees. Innovation can create employment ((Maráková & Medveď'ová, 2010) and long-term economic growth (Rosenberg, 2003): thus, the quality of life will improve in the destination (prosperity).

Additionally, the model of growth of Porter et al. (2000) includes innovation to attain a high economic growth rate. Innovation in technology is an essential component in the model of growth (Romer, 1986), where innovation is an endogenous element in long-run growth.

As Freeman and Soete (1997) comment, innovation is a concept that can make the tourism destination more efficient and technologically advanced, leading to an improvement in the quality of life for the inhabitants and tourists. Thus, prosperity is linked to economic concepts but also to quality of life concepts, such as technological resources (e.g. a smart city), low pollution levels, or anything related to happiness.

Technological innovation makes a relevant contribution to economic development (Romer, 1986). Prosperity can be measured by gross domestic product (GDP) and other variables such as satisfaction or employment (Garcia-Sánchez and Siles, 2015b). Product innovation increases GDP (Rosenberg, 2003). Ulku (2004) observes a positive and significant relation between innovation and GDP.

Innovation must be made sustainably. Hjalager (1997) comments that if a destination innovates but produces contamination in the process, the quality of life will decrease, and the tourists will choose another destination.

The association among these three concepts, namely, competitiveness, innovation, and prosperity, is necessary for a tourism destination: an innovative destination will be more competitive and will earn prosperity (Pavia et al., 2011).

Methodology

To test the validity of the model we set four hypotheses; then, we can check the effects among the constructs and their reliability. In Figure 1, a theoretical model of the relationship of these three elements is presented.

In the model, the three constructs are represented in circles, and each concept is measured by a set of indicators. Following the literature, the arrows indicate the direction of the supposed effect; thus, competitiveness should have a direct effect on prosperity, and innovation should have a direct effect on competitiveness and prosperity.

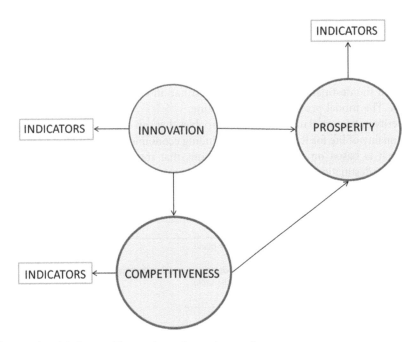

Figure 1. Theoretical model of competitiveness, innovation, and prosperity.

The model produces the following hypotheses:

H_0: Competitiveness has a significative effect on prosperity.

H_1: Innovation has a direct effect on competitiveness.

H_2: Innovation has a meaningful effect on prosperity.

H_3: Innovation as a mediator construct.

The dataset

For this study, data from different statistical sources have been extracted. The sources range from web statistics (e.g. the official statistics institute in Spain or diverse official ministry webs) to relevant surveys (e.g. employment, technological, or tourism surveys) (see Table 1). Cross-sectional data from 2015 has been chosen because this is the final year that the "more updated" data is available. Many variables do not vary across years; thus, this method is suitable for the results we hope to observe.

Spain is a recognized tourist destination. According to the Travel and Tourism Competitiveness Report (World Economic Forum, 2017), regarding 14 pillars of competitiveness indicators, Spain came in first of the 136 countries analysed. Thus, a deep study of tourism will report benefits for tourists and inhabitants at the destination, helping to maintain the tourism share of Spain.

The number of observations is based on the number of provinces. Spain has 52 provinces that comprise diverse tourism typologies, such as sun and sand, mountain, sports, shopping, cultural, and urban.

Competitiveness' indicators have been searched, taking into account relevant tourism competitiveness theory from articles such as Crouch and Ritchie (1999), Dwyer and Kim (2003), and, above all, García-Sánchez and Siles (2015a) that made a deep research of tourism competitiveness' indicators suitable for tourism in Spain.

Tourism competitiveness is presented as a multidimensional concept summarized in blocks of resources made of several indicators. These indicators represent aspects such as natural resources, cultural resources, demand conditions, destination management, supporting resources, and location resources. Qualitative and quantitative data are necessary to assess competitiveness at the destinations (Kozak & Rimmington, 1999). The authors affirm there is no single package of indicators for all the destinations; instead, each destination can have their own, depending on its characteristics. The model provides a general frame.

The prosperity indicators' dataset comprises variables that can create a prosperous destination and offer a better quality of life for its inhabitants, including economic indicators and relevant indicators.

This research is based on important affirmations that tourism researchers have made about prosperity in the destinations. Employment can be an economic indicator to measure prosperity

Table 1. Variables in the model, description, and data sources.

Variables and description	Data sources
Foreign tourism plane: index of foreign tourists arriving by plane	www.fomento.gob.es
Hospitals: number of hospitals	www.msssi.gob.es
Import ind. & tech. good: value in euros of imports of industrial and technology goods	www.icex.es
Industrial employment: number of workers in the industrial sector	www.seg-social.es
Investigation cent.+ 1: number of investigation centres	www.csic.es
Smart city+ 1: number of smart cities	www.redciudadesinteligentes.es
Tech cent.+ 1: number of technology centres	www.fecyt.es
Shop+ 1: number of commercial centres	www.elcorteingles.es
Theme park+ 1: number of theme parks	www.parkscout.es
Univ+ 1: number of universities	www.ua.es

Source: Own elaboration

and improve the workers' quality of life, increase productivity in the destination, and generate consumption through salaries (Craigwell, 2007; Dwyer & Kim, 2003; Dwyer et al., 2003). The added value of the economy's sectors supposes an increase of each sector to the destination's GDP; thus, it will increase the prosperity (Buhalis, 2000; Hong, 2008). GDP and per capita GDP are indicators of quality of life at the destination. The more per capita GDP, more opportunities for study, and more resources the inhabitants will have (Crouch & Ritchie, 1999; Dwyer & Kim, 2003).

Additionally, we must account for every indicator that can make the tourists and the destination's inhabitants feel comfortable and happy at the destination. Therefore, happiness indicators like those used by Croes (2017) (e.g. level of optimism, happiness, and satisfaction with life) or related to rural tourism, environmental indicators (Goh, 2012), or any indicator that can make the way of life better can be valid.

Regarding the innovation indicator's research, it has been performed by following various articles and handbooks about innovation and its development in the destinations. Indicators like R&D expenses, universities, investigation centres, equipment and knowledge acquisition, and innovation policies are described in the Oslo's Manual (OECD, 2005). Industrial development, human resources' training, and new software development are indicators cited in the Frascati's Manual (OECD, 2002). Other indicators related to innovation are detailed in articles such as Adams and Jaffe (1996), Álvarez et al. (2008), Dwyer and Kim (2003), The European Innovation Scoreboard (European Commission, (2016)), Innovation in Spain (FECYT, 2014), Klette (1994), Malinoski and Perry (2011), National Research Council (1997), Puccio and Grana (2008), and Rogers (1998).

An initial dataset of 72 indicators has been disposed for this study: 37 from competitiveness, 21 from innovation, and 14 about prosperity. All the data have been transformed to logarithms; in this way, we eliminate the effect of the different measures from the data and account for only the difference between observations. Additionally, understanding the results from the model is easier because the model measures variance between the latent variables.

Partial least squares methodology

To develop the principal model, we require a second generation technique of multivariate analysis because we have three independent variables that have effects among them. Structural equation modelling (SEM) combines multiple regression with factorial analysis; thus, we can estimate models with several linear regressions and a factorial analysis of the variables in every construct together. SEM estimates and assesses the outer model (i.e. the relationship between indicators and constructs) and inner model (i.e. effect among the constructs).

Partial least squares (PLS) is an SEM technique based on variance commonly used in the literature (Chin, Marcolin, & Newsted, 1996). We have chosen PLS because of its suitability for models with few observations (i.e. between 30 and 100) (Chin, 2010). With this nonparametric technique, we do not have to suppose normality in the entire dataset.

According to Wong (2013), we analyse the model in terms of the inner and outer models, followed by validation tests and other verifications:

In the initial model, we set the variables selected and form three constructs or latent variables. The data set comprises primary and secondary data, and PLS can also be used with secondary data (Latan & Ghozali, 2012). The latent variables are competitiveness, innovation, and prosperity. All three constructs are reflective constructs, and constructs cause the indicators. The variables are interchangeable without changing the construct's concept. The indicators are usually correlated because they are interchangeable, as aforementioned.

Covariation among the indicators are caused by variation in the latent variable; thus, changes in the construct can cause changes in the indicators, but not the other way around (Jarvis, Mackenzie, & Podsakoff, 2003).

Results

After identifying the variables that can form every construct from the literature review, we dispose them in the general model as part of every latent variable. Checking the results, we can make the following statements: first, the algorithm converged after 17 iterations from a maximum of 300; thus, it is a satisfactory estimation. The coefficient of determination R^2 is 0.712 for the endogenous latent variable prosperity. The two latent variables, namely, competitiveness and innovation, explain 71.2% of the variance in prosperity. Innovation explains 76.4% of the variance in competitiveness.

Using this method, we must quit various indicators, probably because the number of observations available is insufficient for a model with 72 variables, in which one of the constructs is defined by 37 variables. The software SmartPLS builds every construct with a few indicators that are sufficient to represent the concept. In reflective models, the indicators are highly correlated and interchangeable (Wong, 2013). The final 10 indicators and their definitions are detailed in Table 1.

Competitiveness comprises services indicators (supporting factors in the integrated model) such as hospitals. The cultural indicator is represented by universities (endowed resources). The leisure indicators (created resources) comprises, for example, shops and theme parks. The market performance indicator is the foreign share of tourists that come by plane. The innovation construct comprises technological centres, investigation centres, and equipment goods purchases. Finally, prosperity is defined by industrial sector employment and living in a smart city.

As aforementioned, PLS is more suitable for small samples (Reinartz, Haenlein, & Henseler, 2009), and we have a reduced dataset that follows the rule of 10. Thus, the number of observations must be 10 times higher than the maximum number of arrows that one construct receives for having a significance level of 0.5 and statistical power of 0.8. Our dataset comprises 52 observations; following the rule, there must be over 50 for it to be valid.

After we run the final model, the results are as follows: the algorithm converged after 6 iterations from a maximum of 300; it is a satisfactory estimation. The results of the PLS algorithm are presented in Figure 2.

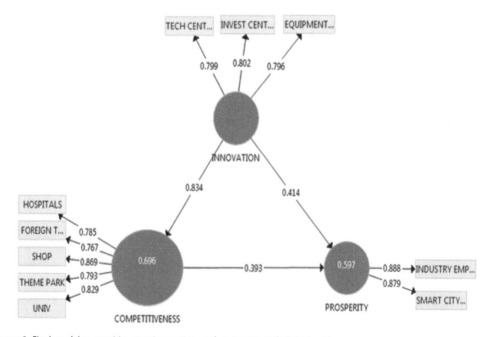

Figure 2. Final model competitiveness, innovation, and prosperity with PLS algorithm.

The coefficient of determination R^2 is 0.597 for the endogenous latent variable prosperity. The two latent variables competitiveness and innovation explain 59.7% of the variance in prosperity; it is a moderate result. Innovation explains 69.6% of the variance in competitiveness. Values above 0.36 are high (Wetzels, Odekerken-Schröder, & Van-Oppen, 2009). Chin (1998) said that approximately 0.67 is a high value.

The inner model suggests that innovation still has a strong effect on competitiveness (0.834). The hypothesized path relationship between innovation and competitiveness is statistically significative. Innovation has a moderate effect on prosperity (0.414). The hypothesized path relationship between innovation and prosperity is statistically significative. Competitiveness has a moderate effect on prosperity (0.393), but this is lower than innovation. The hypothesized path relationship between competitiveness and prosperity is statistically significative. As Chin (1998, p. XIII) affirms: standardized paths should be approximately 0.2 and ideally above 0.3 to be considered meaningful.

We must square each of the outer loadings to find the indicator reliability value: 0.70 or higher is preferred. Inexploratory research, 0.4 or higher is acceptable. (Hair, Ringle, & Sarstedt, 2013; Hulland, 1999). Loadings of 0.5 or 0.6 may be acceptable (Chin, 2010).

All the loadings are greater than 0.707, as Chin (2010, p. 685) suggests is ideal. The loadings of the final model are disposed in Table 2.

Our model is an exploratory model because we attempt to prove if innovation is a construct. Theoretically, innovation is part of competitiveness, and we have a background regarding competitiveness, its indicators, and its incidence on prosperity; however, in this article, we explore the possibility that innovation is a third construct with its own indicators that have significative incidence on both competitiveness and prosperity, and theoretical knowledge in this assumption is limited (Chin, 2010). For that reason, we affirm that we are working with an exploratory model and will select indicators with squared loadings higher than 0.4.

In the model presented, the indicators with a higher incidence in competitiveness are cultural indicators (universities), followed by leisure indicators (shops and theme parks), services indicators (hospitals), and market performance indicators (foreign share). The most important indicators for innovation are investigation centres, technological centres, and the importation of equipment goods. The prosperity of the destinations is important to the employment of the industrial sector, employment provides additional resources to inhabitants and generates consumption and living in a smart city.

The validity of the model is tested with relevant indicators. Table 2 also indicates that all the indicators have individual indicator reliability values larger than the minimum accepted 0.4 and are much closer to the preferred level of 0.7. Cronbach's alpha is used to measure internal consistency reliability, and composite reliability can be also used (Hair, Sarstedt, Ringle, & Mena, 2012). All values obtained are larger than 0.6; thus, high levels of internal consistency reliability have been demonstrated among the three reflective latent variables. Cronbach's alpha is greater than 0.7 (Hair et al., 2013) anyway.

To check convergent validity, average variance extracted (AVE) from each latent variable must be greater than 0.5 (Hair et al., 2013). All values presented are greater than this threshold.

Table 2. Results of the model.

LATENT VARIABLE	INDICATORS	LOAD.	IND. REL.	COMP. REL.	AVE	CR. ALPHA	AVE SQ. R.
Competitive-ness	Foreign tourism	0.767	0.588	0.905	0.655	0.868	0.809
	Hospitals	0.785	0.616				
	Shopping Centre	0.869	0.755				
	Theme park	0.793	0.629				
	Universities	0.829	0.687				
Innovation	Equipment	0.796	0.634	0.841	0.639	0.717	0.799
	Research centre	0.802	0.643				
	Tech. cent.	0.799	0.638				
Prosperity	Ind. employ.	0.888	0.789	0.877	0.781	0.720	0.884
	Smart city	0.879	0.773				

Discriminant validity is checked following Fornell & Larcker's (1981) criterium of the squared root of AVE. This value must be larger than other correlation values among the latent variables. Discriminant validity is well established in the cases of innovation and prosperity. In the case of competitiveness, the squared root of AVE is very close to the correlation between competitiveness and innovation, and we can interpret that as innovation highly related with competitiveness because it is a concept that enhances competitiveness and a variable that has been part of competitiveness before; this study will demonstrate the importance of innovation on its own for prosperity.

We use a bootstrapping process to check the significance of the inner and outer models with a T-statistics test. The test is a two-tailed T test with a significance level of 5%. The path coefficient is significant if the T-statistics test is larger than 1.96. In our model, the path coefficients between innovation and competitiveness, between innovation and prosperity, and between competitiveness and prosperity are significative at a 5% level. In the outer model, the T-statistics test for the variables presents all the results significative at a 1% level.

To avoid the collinearity problem, variance inflation factor values must be 5 or lower (Hair, Ringle, & Sarstedt, 2011). In our model, all the values in the inner and outer models are lower than 5.

The f^2 effect measures how much the exogenous latent variable contributes to an endogenous latent variable's R^2 value (the strength of the relationship between the latent variables) (Chin et al., 1996). The values of 0.02, 0.15, and 0.35 mean a small, medium, or large effect, respectively (Chin, 2010; Cohen, 1988). The values of that effect in the inner model are medium for the relationship between competitiveness and prosperity, and innovation and prosperity. The value is high for the relationship between innovation and competitiveness.

In addition to considering R^2 as a criterion for predictive relevance of the inner model, Chin (2010) suggests that the Stone-Geisser's Q^2 can also be applied. The blindfolding process shows results higher than 0, except for innovation because innovation is a latent variable not affected by others; thus, the model has predictive relevance for the latent variables.

The results from the tests performed confirm the first three hypotheses. The last hypothesis indicates the importance of analysing the mediation effects on the structural model to obtain a more complete picture of the cause–effect relationships between constructs (Hair et al., 2013); a bootstrapping analysis is especially valuable.

The total effects are the sum of the direct effects and indirect effects. Thus, the analysis of the total effects we have performed shows that the total effects are statistically significative (P value < 0.001) between the constructs innovation–competitiveness and innovation–prosperity, but the effect is weaker between competitiveness and prosperity (P value < 0.05). The indirect effects show a weak indirect effect of innovation on prosperity (P value < 0.05). Although innovation is an important factor for prosperity, a stronger direct effect exists between these two constructs. We conclude that the model is well formed, and all the effects have positive coefficients; however, the mediation effect is not strong. The total effects analysis demonstrates the constructs are related, and this result is crucial to specifying that this relationship that can be predictive, as Söllner, Bitzer, Janson, and Leimeister (2018) indicate.

Conclusion and implications

Tourism competitiveness is a relevant concept for the destinations that want to increase their prosperity. The study of the competitiveness of the destinations analysed should lead to better management of the destination through a model that can confirm the importance of each aspect of competitiveness.

Notably, García-Sánchez and Siles (2015a) has been updated and can confirm the same relationship between competitiveness and prosperity in Spain's destinations. We have used different indicators, but ours represent the same concepts of how competitiveness can be defined.

Using a PLS model has helped us develop a model with various relationships among the constructs. The dataset design is suitable to be implemented as a structural equation model and is an easy way to describe our theoretical model empirically.

The number of observations does not allow us to obtain results for the entire dataset; thus, a more reduced model is presented. This model represents the concepts we want to present. The results are robust, and the tests realized verify the suitability of the model.

The relationship between innovation and competitiveness is strong, and this is reasonable because innovation has a significant effect on competitiveness. The relationship between competitiveness and prosperity, which has been demonstrated in the literature, is confirmed anew with a moderate effect. Finally, the effect of innovation on prosperity is proven with a moderate significance.

In this article, the suitability of innovation as a third construct is proven, obtaining prosperity and competitiveness for the destinations analysed. Innovation is more than a variable of competitiveness and has significative effects on prosperity. Mediation effects of innovation have been analysed, and the result is not conclusive.

The implications of innovation as a concept that can generate prosperity directly must be considered to implement innovation at the destinations. Innovation is introduced with the aim of lifting the quality of life of the inhabitants and the tourists visiting the destination, but sustainability should be considered when innovating, making the tourist experience more satisfactory.

Additional research in this direction can be performed in the future. A more complete model with a higher number of observations would be desirable. We should consider other concepts that can strengthen the effect of innovation on prosperity. Thus, a deeper analysis of which innovation indicators are more suitable for obtaining higher levels of prosperity could be realized for the destinations analysed.

The study confirms a novel model of competitiveness, innovation, and prosperity, and the necessary association of these three concepts for a prosperous tourism destination.

Disclosure statement

No potential conflict of interest was reported by the authors.

References

Adams, J., & Jaffe, A. (1996). Bounding the effects of R&D: An investigation using Matched establishment-firm data. *Rand Journal of Economics*, *27*, 700–721.

Álvarez, S. A., Rego, V. G., Leira, L. J., Gomis, R. A., Caramés, V. R., & Andrade, S. M. J. (2008). Innovación turística: perspectivas teóricas y objetos de estudio [tourism innovation: theoretical perspectives]. *Revista De Ocio Y Turismo*, *1*(19–50). doi:10.17979/rotur.2008.1.1.1224

Buhalis, D. (1998). Strategic use of information technology in the tourism industry. *Tourism Management*, *19*(5), 409–421.

Buhalis, D. (2000). Marketing the competitive destinations of the future. *Tourism Management*, *21*, 97–116.

Bulc, V. (2011). Innovation ecosystem and tourism. *Academia Turística*, *4*(1), 27–34.

Cadavid, H. J. V., & Franco, G. H. (2006). Factores determinantes de la relación entre el crecimiento económico, la equidad y la competitividad [factors determining the relationship among economic growth, equity and competitiveness]. *Ecos De Economía, 23*, 107–153.

Chin, W. W., Marcolin, B. L., & Newsted, P. R. (1996). A partial least squares latent variable modelling approach for measuring interaction effects: results from a monte carlo simulation study and voice mail emotion/adoption study. in J. I. DeGross, S. Jarvenpaa, & A. Srinivasan (Eds.) *Proceedings of the Seventeenth International Conference on Information Systems* (pp. 21–41).

Chin, W. W. (1998). *Issues and Opinions on Structural Equation Modelling. MIS Quarterly, 22*(1), VII–XVI.

Chin, W. W. (2010). How to write and report PLS analyses. In V. Esposito Vinzi, W. W. Chin, J. Henseler, & H. Wang (Eds.), *Handbook of partial least squares: concepts, methods and applications (springer handbooks of computational Statistics Series* (Vol. II, pp. 655–690). Springer, Heidelberg.

Cohen, J. (1988). *Statistical Power Analysis for the Behavioural Sciences* (2nd ed.). New Jersey: Lawrence Erlbaum Associates.

Council, N. R. (1997). *Industrial Research and Innovation Indicators: Report of a Workshop.* Washington, DC: The National Academies Press. doi: 10.17226/5976.

Craigwell, R. (2007). *Tourism Competitiveness in Small Island Developing State.* Research Paper 2007/19 United Nations University, World Institute for Development Economics Research, Helsinki: Finland.

Croes, R. (2017). *Happiness and Tourism: Evidence from Aruba. The Dick Pope Sr. Institute for Tourism Studies.* Orlando: Florida.

Crouch, G. I., & Ritchie, J. R. B. (1999). Tourism, competitiveness, and societal prosperity. *Journal of Business Research, 44*, 137–152.

Dwyer, L., & Kim, C. (2003). Destination competitiveness: Determinants and indicators. *Current Issues in Tourism, 6*(5), 369–414.

Dwyer, L., Livaic, Z., & Mellor, R. (2003). Competitiveness of Australia as a tourist destination. *Journal of Hospitality and Tourism Management, 10*(1), 60–79.

Dwyer, L., Mellor, R., Livaic, Z., Edwards, D., & Kim, C. (2004). Attributes of destination competitiveness: A factor analysis. *Tourism Analysis, 9*(1–2), 91–101.

Esteban, A. (2005). *La Demanda de Servicios Culturales: Aspectos Motivacionales y Funcionales del Consumidor de Turismo Cultural [The demand for cultural services: Motivational and functional aspects of cultural tourists]. Gestión del Turismo Cultural y de Ciudad.* España: ediciones de la Universidad de Castilla La Mancha, pp. 95-114), Cuenca.

European Commission. (2016). *European Innovation Scoreboard 2016.* Belgium: European Union.

FECYT. (2014). *La Innovación en España según el Cuadro de Indicadores de la Unión por la Innovación [Innovation in Spain according to the Table of Indicators of the Union for Innovation].* Spain: Fundación Española para la Ciencia y la Tecnología.

Fornell, C., & Larcker, D. F. (1981). Evaluating Structural Equation Models with unobservable variables and measurement error. *Journal of Marketing Research, 18*(1), 39–50.

Forum, W. E., *The Travel & Tourism Competitiveness Report* 2017. Retrieved from https://www.weforum.org/reports/the-travel-tourism-competitiveness-report-2017

Freeman, C., & Soete, L. (1997). The Economics of Industrial Innovation. In *Mit Press.* Cambridge: USA.

García-Sánchez, A., & Siles, D. (2015b). Tourism destination competitiveness and Innovation: The case of the Spanish Mediterranean Coast. A. Artal-Tul & M. Kozak Eds.. *Destination Competitiveness, The Environment and Sustainability* . CAB International. Wallingford: UK. 13–23.

García-Sánchez, A., & Siles, D. (2015a). Tourism destination competitiveness: The Spanish Mediterranean case. *Tourism Economics, 21*(6), 1235–1254.

Goh, C. (2012). Exploring impact of climate on tourism demand. *Annals of Tourism Research, 39*(4), 1859–1883.

Hair, J. F., Ringle, C. M., & Sarstedt, M. (2011). PLS-SEM: Indeed a silver bullet. *Journal of Marketing Theory and Practice, 19*(2), 139–151.

Hair, J. F., Ringle, C. M., & Sarstedt, M. (2013). Partial least squares structural equation modelling: rigorous applications, better results, and higher acceptance. *Long Range Planning, 46*, 1–12. doi: 10.1016/j.lrp.2013.01.001.

Hair, J. F., Sarstedt, M., Ringle, C. M., & Mena, J. A. (2012). An Assessment of the use of Partial Least Squares Structural Equation Modelling in marketing research. *Journal of the Academy of Marketing Science, 40*(3), 414–433.

Hjalager, A. M. (1997). Innovation patterns in sustainable tourism. *Tourism Management, 18*(1), 35–41.

Hjalager, A. M. (2010). A review of innovation research in tourism. *Tourism Management, 31*, 1–12.

Hong, W. (2008). *Competitiveness in Tourism Sector: A Comprehensive Approach from Economic and Management Points Physica-Verlag.* Heidelberg: Germany.

Hu, M. M., Horng, J., & Sun, Y. C. (2009). Hospitality teams: Knowledge sharing and service innovation performance. *Tourism Management, 30*, 41–50.

Hulland, J. (1999). Use of Partial Least Squares (PLS) in strategic management research: A review of four recent studies. *Strategic Management Journal, 20*(2), 195–204.

Jarvis, C. B., Mackenzie, S. B., & Podsakoff, P. M. (2003). A critical review of construct indicators and measurement model misspecification in marketing and consumer research. *Journal of Consumer Research, 30*(2), 199–218.

Klette, J. (1994). *R&D, Scope Economies and Company Structure: A "Not-so-Fixed Effect" Model of Plant Performance. Discussion Paper s.* Research Department: 120. Statistics Norway. doi:10.2307/2555841

Kozak, M., & Rimmington, M. (1999). Measuring tourist destination competitiveness: Conceptual considerations and empirical findings. *International Journal of Hospitality Management, 18,* 273–283.

Latan, H., & Ghozali, I. (2012). *Partial Least Squares: Concept, Technique and Application SmartPLS 2.0 M3.* Semarang: Badan Penerbit Universitas Diponegoro.

Malinoski, M., & Perry, G. S. (2011). *How do I measure "Innovation"?!?* Balanced Scorecard Institute, a Strategy Management Group company. Cary, North Carolina: US. Retrieved from http://www.balancedscorecard.org/portals/0/pdf/Howtomeasureinnovation.pdf

Maráková, V., & Medved'ová, M. (2010). Innovation in Tourism Destinations. *Forum Scientiae Oeconomia, 4*(1), 33–43.

Meneses, O., & Teixeira, A. (2011). The innovative behaviour of tourism firms. *Economics and Management Research Projects: an International Journal, 1*(1), 25–35.

Newall, J. E. (1992). The Challenge of Competitiveness.*The Business Quarterly,* 56 (4): 94–100.

OECD. (2002). *Frascati manual, proposed standard practice for surveys research and experimental development.* Paris: Author.

OECD. (2005). *Oslo Manual: Guidelines for Collecting and Interpreting Innovation Data* (3rd ed.). Paris: Author.

Pavia, N., Stipanovic, C., & Mrnjavac, E. (2011). Innovation of business culture with the aim of developing croatian tourism-case study of Valamar hotels and resorts. *Academia Turística, 4*(1), 95–102.

Perna, F., Custódio, M. J., & Oliveira, V. (2018). Tourism destination competitiveness: An application model for the south of Portugal versus the Mediterranean region of Spain: COMPEITITIVTOUR. *Tourism and Management Studies, 14*(1), 19–29.

Porter, M. E. (1990). *The Competitive Advantage of Nations.* New York: Free Press.

Porter, M. E., Sachs, J. D., & McArthur, J. W. (2001). *Executive summary: Competitiveness and Stages of Economic Development. The Global Competitiveness Report 2001-2002, The World Economic Forum* (pp. 16–25). Oxford, New York: Oxford University Press.

Porter, M. E., Sachs, J. D., & Warner, A. M. (2000). *Executive summary: Current Competitiveness and Growth Competitiveness. The Global Competitiveness Report 2000, TheWorld Economic Forum* (pp. 14–17). Oxford, New York: Oxford University Press.

Puccio, H., & Grana, N. (2008). La Innovación como Requisito para la Competitividad Turística [Innovation as a prerequisite for tourism competitiveness]. *Gestión Turística, 10,* 59–76.

Pulido, F. J. I., & Sánchez-Rivero, M. (2010). Competitividad Versus Crecimiento en Destinos Turísticos. Un Análisis mediante Técnicas Multivariantes [Competitiveness versus growth at tourism destinations: A multivariate approach]. *Cuadernos De Economía, 33*(91), 159–181.

Reinartz, W., Haenlein, M., & Henseler, J. (2009). An empirical comparison of the efficacy of covariance-based and variance-based SEM. *Internal Journal of Research in Marketing, 26*(332–344). doi:10.1016/j.ijresmar.2009.08.001

Ritchie, J. R. B., & Crouch, G. I. (2003). *The Competitive Destination: A Sustainable Tourism Perspective.* CABI: Oxford. doi:10.1079/9780851996646.0000

Rogers, M. (1998). The definition and measurement of innovation. *Melbourne Institute Working Paper* 10/98.

Romer, P. M. (1986). Increasing returns and long-run growth. *The Journal of Political Economy, 94*(5), 1002–1037.

Rosenberg, N. (2003). *Innovation and Economic Growth.* OECD Conference of Innovation and Growth in Tourism. Lugano: Switzerland, 18–19 September.

Rosenberg, N. (2006). Innovation and Economic Growth. In *Innovation and Growth in Tourism.* Paris: OECD Publications.

Sancho, P. A. (2008). Innovación Tecnológica, Competitividad y Productividad: Una Aproximación al Sector Hostelería y Restauración de la Comunidad Valenciana [Technological innovation, competitiveness and productivity: An approach for the hospitality sector in Valencia región, Spain]. *Revista De Ocio Y Turismo, 1,* 153–164.

Sancho, P. A., & Maset, L. A. (1999). Sector Turístico e Innovación: Un Análisis a través de Patentes [Tourism sector and Innovation: A patent-based analysis]. In *I Congreso Nacional Turismo y Tecnologías de la Información y las Comunicaciones: Nuevas Tecnologías y Calidad* (pp. 249–261). CEDMA, Málaga: Spain.

Scott, B. R., & Lodge, G. C. (1985). *U.S. Competitiveness in the World Economy.* Boston: US: Harvard Business School Press.

Söllner, M, Bitzer, P, Janson, A, & Leimeister, J.M. (2018). Process is king: evaluating the performance of technology-mediated learning in vocational software training. *Journal of Information Technology, 33*(3), 233–253. doi: 10.1057/s41265-017-0046-6

Sundbo, J., Orfila-Sintes, F., & Sorensen, F. (2007). The innovative behaviour of tourism firms-comparative studies of Denmark and Spain. *Research Policy, 36,* 88–106.

Travel, W., & Council, T. (2017). *Economic Impact.* Retrieved from https://www.wttc.org/research/economic-research/economic-impact-analysis/

Ulku, H. (2004). *R&D, Innovation, and Economic Growth: An Empirical Analysis.* IMF Working papers 04/185. International Monetary Fund. Washington DC: US.

Victorino, L., Verma, R., Plaschaka, F., & Dev, C. (2005). Service innovation and customer choices in the hospitality industry. *Managing Service Quality*, *15*(6), 555–576.

Wetzels, M., Odekerken-Schröder, G., & Van-Oppen, C. (2009). Using PLS Path Modelling for assessing hierarchical construct models: Guidelines and empirical illustration. *MIS Quarterly*, *33*(1), 177–195.

Wong, K. K. (2013). Partial Least Squares Structural Equation Modelling (PLS-SEM) Techniques Using SmartPLS. *Marketing Bulletin*, *24*, 1–32.

Wysokinska, Z. (2003). Competitiveness and its relationships with productivity and sustainable development. *Fibre and Textiles in Eastern Europe*, *11*(3), 11–14.

Recreational value of El Valle and Carrascoy Natural Park

Miguel Ángel Tobarra-González and Javier Mendoza-Monpeán

ABSTRACT

In this paper, an estimate of recreational value of El Valle and Carrascoy Natural Park is obtained by applying individual travel cost method. A consumer surplus or benefit of one visit (of one person) to this natural park has been estimated in 5.09 euros. This figure can provide information to stakeholders in order to determine recreational investments and to get a proper environment management and sustainable use of this place. As the model shows, people react to travel cost, and so, an entrance fee would reduce the number of visits in case of overcrowding. Nonetheless, given the profile of visitor, signalling and information about a proper use from an environmental point of view would be a socially preferable policy.

Introduction

Tourism has become an important economic sector but has also caused several unwanted economic, environmental and sociocultural impacts (Briassoulis, 2003). Problems as seasonality (Butler, 1994), overcrowding (Brouwer, Turner, & Voisey, 2001), water scarcity for local people (Cole, 2014) or local community annoyances (Lai & Hitchcock, 2017), between many others, have been recovered in the literature.

Environmental impacts of tourism are especially important since natural resources are limited and environment is also an important tourist attractiveness. There are many articles that study environmental problems related to tourism and some examples are going to be mentioned below. Araña and León (2016) used a field experiment to test the effectiveness of both non-market and market based sustainability policies in reducing overall CO_2 emission levels by affecting destination choice. Kuvan (2010) emphasises that monitoring and eliminating the negative environmental impacts of tourism is crucial for the protection and continuity of forest resources. Mejía and Sylvia Brandt (2017) say that the increase in demand for nature-based tourism brings economic and educational benefits but risks the introduction of invasive species. Moorhouse, D' Cruze, and Macdonald (2017) point out unethical use of wildlife.

Ecotourism, nature-based and rural tourism are products that have grown steadily during last years. All of them have the nature, and especially natural parks, as core resources. Natural areas can feel the impact of human activity when tourism develops and problems of sustainability can emerge in these areas (Fleming & Manning, 2015). At the same time, nature-based tourism can be one mean to help to achieve sustainability in the reserve areas (Salam, Lindsay, & Beveridge, 2000). So, investment on environmental quality can be necessary for a good management of environment and tourism.

El Valle and Carrascoy is a natural park located in the southeast of Spain, with an increasing number of visitors given that it is closely located to important population centres. It is a recreational area with an important environmental value. In this natural park, as in many others all around the world, it is necessary that managers and institutions got to make the recreational use of these reserve areas compatible with their environmental conservation. One issue that can help in the achievement of environmental preservation is knowing the richness and value of natural parks. This paper estimates the recreational value of El Valle and Carrascoy Natural Park, what can help to its tourist management and also to increase consciousness of surrounding population and institutions on the its environmental value. Individual travel cost methodology has been applied using data from questionnaires put in 2016 to a sample of 215 visitors. As a result, careful information is provided to authorities that manage this natural resource, what can help them to rely on cost-benefit analysis when designing policies regarding such a natural place.

Literature review

Natural parks are used by visitors that frequently cause a negative impact. The value of these places and the possible damage caused by tourism is an important issue to be taken into account in tourism management (Palmer & Riera, 2003). Recent tourism studies have incorporated economic methods in order to attain valuation of environmental goods and damages, that do not have structured markets from which a market price, and hence, a reference market value could be obtained (Tisdell, 2004).

Economic analysis approaches these issues by relying on a number of valuation methods (Folmer & Ierland, 1989). They can be divided into two big groups: direct or stated preferences methods (as contingent valuation or choice experiments) and indirect or revealed preferences methods (as travel cost or hedonic prices).

Directs methods obtain the value of an environmental good or a change in its supply through a direct statement of people. In them, a market is simulated. For example, in the contingent valuation method that uses a dichotomous answer in the valuation question, interviewed people are asked if they would pay a determined price for a good or an environmental improvement. Interviewee would say "yes" if the value of this improvement for him/her was greater than the cost (or price) suggested and would say "no" in the opposite case. It is as a hypothetical or simulated market. From these responses a valuation can be obtained through statistical technics (Haneman, 1984).

Indirect methods obtain information from markets of goods that are related to the good whose value is trying to be determined. For example, travel cost method gets a valuation of a good from information about the cost of travel necessary to enjoy it.

These environmental economic methods have been incorporated in tourism studies, especially direct methods that have been used by Báez-Montenedro, Bedate Centeno, Sanz Lara, and Herrero Prieto (2015), Baral, Kaul, Heinen, and Ale (2017), Casey, Brown, and Schuhmann (2010), Chiou, Lin, Liu, and Lin (2016), Choi and Ritchie (2014), Hergesell and Dickinger (2013), Lee, Lee, Kim & Mjelde (2010), Saayman and Saayman (2017), and Wuepper (2016). Indirect method seems to be less used and only Mangan, Brouwer, Lohano, and Nangraj (2013), Riera Font (2000), and Wallentin (2016) are cited in this paper.

Casey et al. (2010) use a discrete choice contingent valuation experiment with almost 400 visitors to determine a measure of compensating variation for contributing to a public trust to protect corals. They estimate a mean willingness to pay (WTP) of over $55.00. These results suggest that there are significant possibilities for implementing a "coral fund" to raise revenues for coral protection programmes in the Riviera Maya region of Mexico's Yucatan Peninsula. Lee, Lee, Kim, and Mjelde (2010) identify the activity and experience preferences of bird-watchers; they use choice experiment methods to estimate their willingness to pay for bird-watching-related ecotourism tour and interpretive services. Hergesell and Dickinger (2013) investigate the role of price, time and convenience regarding transport mode choice using a stated choice experiment. They used data from 372 European students resulting in 5952 choice situations and concluded that cost is the most important product attribute followed by time, with convenience playing a secondary role for student travellers. Mangan et al. (2013) estimated recreational value of Keenjhar Lake in Pakistan using a travel cost model.

Saayman and Saayman (2017) used contingent valuation method to obtain the non-consumptive value or the appreciative value of the rhino, based on three surveys conducted in South Africa's Kruger National Park (KNP) from 2011 to 2013. They affirm that the non-consumptive value is greater than the consumptive value of rhino that is driven by the hunting price. Choi and Ritchie (2014) developed and applied a choice modelling study to measure the economic values of aviation carbon mitigation and to identify major factors influencing air travellers' voluntary climate action.

Results show that respondents have a mean willingness to pay (WTP) of AU$21.38 per tonne of CO_2 reduced in the form of voluntary carbon offsets per person. Báez-Montenedro et al. (2015) determine the economic value assigned to the historical heritage of Valdivia (Chile) by tourists visiting the city using contingent valuation method. Chiou et al. (2016) applied contingent valuation method to evaluate the benefits of protective forests. For it, they used the willingness to pay for entrance to the Taitung Forest Park, that was estimated in NT$21.7 for each person. Wallentin (2016) proposes a novel aggregated zonal travel cost model for estimating demand for a single recreation site when data are limited. Wuepper (2016) uses a choice experiment to value the World Heritage status for a German natural park. They find a per-person increase in willingness to pay of €4.70 which translates into an overall value increase of €3.8 million annually. Baral et al. (2017) estimate the economic value of World Heritage Site (WHS) designation for the Sagarmatha (Mount Everest) National Park, in Nepal, using the contingent valuation method. They obtained that median WTP amount was US $90.93 per trip and 63.8% of visitors were willing to pay more than the existing entry.

El Valle and Carrascoy: a natural park in the Southeast of Spain

El Valle and Carrascoy Natural Park is located in the southeast of Spain with an area of 17,410 ha that are spread about the municipalities of Murcia, Fuente Álamo and Alhama in the Region of Murcia, Spain. It's a natural park closely linked to local population, given its proximity to the city of Murcia and other villages and constitutes the major green lung in this area. Historical heritage resources starting from the Bronze Age, and passing through Iberian, Roman, Arab and Visigoth eras confers this area a huge historic, cultural and religious importance. It is part of Natura 2000 as a Site of Community Importance and Special Protection Area for birds sightseeing due to the presence of eagle owl among others species (Madrigal de Torres, 2015).

Land use corresponds to pasture (54%), forest (33%), fruit trees (6%) and other uses (7%). Agricultural use is decreasing; dry farming is located in flanks of hills and small basins between mountains and there are also some small areas of irrigated land in the west part. Goat and sheep farms are token although there is a potential for small game hunting. Mines exploitation (iron, copper and plaster) stopped in 1993 except small limestone production for construction and ornamentation. Nowadays, recreational use predominates in this site, especially in El Valle and Majal Blanco areas. There are historic remains as Iberian Sanctuary of the Light or the Arab Castle of La Asomada. The catholic Sanctuary of La Fuensanta is also a religious reference here; it was begun to be built in 1694 in baroque style and inside there are interesting pictures and reliefs. It is catalogued as a national monument. There exist five geologic interest places and some facilities for recreational use as an environmental education centre, parking, flora and fauna observatory, visitor centre, a youth hostel, a tree nursery, a botanic garden and recreational area. Guided visits are also organised. There is a wide net of signalled paths all through this natural area, with a total signalled length of 60 km that includes a long route path (GR250 Cartagena-Caravaca de la Cruz) that travel around the park 11 km.

There are 18 different kinds of habitats of interest according to the European Union catalogue. Five of them, that occupy two thirds of the whole park, are included in Annex 1 of EU Habitat Directive since they are considered priority. There exists 55 species of catalogued plants, 48 of them included in the Regional Catalogue of Protected Wild Flora of the Region of Murcia; 33 are considered as species of special interest, 11 are considered as vulnerable and 4 in danger of extinction in the Region of Murcia. This park also has great fauna diversity due to the different vegetation structures arising. Birds constitute the most important group and some species are included in Annex 1 of Directive 79/409/ CEE as golden eagle, real owl, peregrine falcon, short-toed eagle, wheatear or Bonelli's eagle (Alcón-Provencio, Martínez-Paz, Contreras-López, & Navarro-Pay, 2015).

This natural area represents the regional environmental richness and provides cultural, recreational and environmental services that are very valued by local society. As a public good, despite of its owner of property, is a patrimony of all the citizens. So, it is important to know and quantify its social value and particularly its recreational value. In the next section the methodology used to attain this target is exposed.

Methodology

The travel cost method is going to be used in this article to estimate the recreational value of El Valle and Carrascoy Natural Park. This method was firstly proposed by the prize novel Harold Hotelling, based on the surveys of Dupuit, giving rise to zonal travel cost method with equidistance. Different variants of the method has been used in environmental economics for over forty years.

The travel cost method allows estimation of the monetary value of non-marketed goods and services based on revealed preferences and is generally considered the most appropriate method to value recreational experiences (Haab & McConnell, 2002). It is based on the hypothesis that the expenditures made by the visitor to a recreational site, such as travel costs and entrance fees, can be used as surrogate prices to estimate the non-existent prices for their recreational experience (Perman, Ma, McGilvary, & Common, 2003).

Different concepts can be included in the cost of the travel. Between them the fuel expense or transport tickets, travel time, meal, overnight stay or the time of the visit. There is no unanimity between the authors about what of the mentioned concepts should be included in the travel cost except fuel or transport expense.

Travel cost method has several variants, zonal with equidistance, zonal without equidistance and individual (Riera, García, Kriström, & Brännlund, 2005). The individual travel cost model has a number of advantages compared with the zonal travel cost model, including theoretical consistency in modelling individual behaviour and preference heterogeneity, avoidance of arbitrary zone definitions and statistical efficiency in estimating the choice model (Parsons, 2003). Individual method considers individual data of visitors and the variable number of travel made in a determined period is a key variable. A function in which the number of travels in a period of time is explained by travel costs and other explicative variables is specified. A lineal function in which travel cost is the only explicative variable besides the constant is the easiest. Nonetheless, a Poisson or Negative Binomial model is normally used since they can reflect that number of travels/visits variable is not a continuous variable but a discrete one.

In statistical terms, Poisson model supposes a distribution of the kind

$$f(\text{Travels}) = \frac{e^{(\lambda)}\lambda^{\text{Travels}}}{\text{Travels!}} \qquad (1)$$

Where Travels! is factorial of the number of travels or visits made by a visitor during last year and λ is a value such that $\ln \lambda = a + b\text{cost}$, being λ the average of the number of visits, cost, the cost of the travel and ln, natural logarithm function. Once "a" and "b" parameters are estimated, consumer surplus associated to one visit can be obtained as $1/b$.

In our survey, non-visitors are not included in the sample, and therefore, the sample is truncated at zero. Taking into account that this fact can lead to biased and inconsistent estimates due to misspecification of the conditional mean, a zero-truncated Poisson model is going to be used to tackle this issue.

In this survey, the following truncated Poisson model is estimated

$$\Pr(\text{Travels}_i = n \ \text{Ct}_i, \ X_i) = \frac{e^{(-\lambda_i)}\lambda_i^n}{n!(1-e^{-\lambda_i})}, n = 1, 2 \qquad (2)$$

Where travel is the number of visits to the park made by the interviewed person during the last year, n is the number of observed visits for individual "i", Cost_i is the travel cost for individual i, X_i is a vector of characteristics of individual i, and

$$\lambda_i \equiv E(\text{Travels}_i \ n \ \text{Cost}_i, \ X_i) = \exp(\beta\text{Cost}_i + \gamma X_i) \qquad (3)$$

where β y γ are parameters to estimate. Hellerstein and Mendelson (1993) showed that consumer surplus can be obtained from the estimate of the average of the number of travels λ and β parameter, as λ/β.

Data are obtained from a sample of 215 visitors chosen randomly in different parts of El Valle and Carrascoy Natural Park during the months of June and July of 2016. A structured questionnaire was used consisting of questions as the number of visits made during last year, recreational activities developed in the park, travel mode and expenditure associated, level of satisfaction of the visit or socioeconomic characteristics of interviewed person. All the interviewed visitors affirmed to have travelled to engage in recreational activities and did not visit any other site. A large majority revealed to have visited the park before. The visit used to last one morning or one afternoon.

Results

An estimate of recreational value of El Valle and Carrascoy Natural Park is obtained by applying individual travel cost method. The sample characteristics will be commented before explaining the econometric results.

The typical visitor has previously enjoyed the area since 97% of the interviewed people stated having been previously and only 3% were visiting it for the first time. A high repetition rate exists since 60% of the sample stated to have visited the park more than 14 times during last year. This means that this park is very frequented by people living in the surrounding areas that use it as a recreational place. People access to the park mainly by car but also on food and by bicycle. Principal activities during the visit are hill walking (87%), sightseeing (47%), having a picnic (40%) and flora and fauna observation (36%).

The level of satisfaction related to access, signposting, cleanness, flora and fauna, and general satisfaction was asked. Visitors are generally satisfied but cleanness and signposting received worse valuation than the others items. There was an open question about improvements in the park and a high percentage of visitors pointed two issues: signage on the trails and use indications that promoted users respect and conservation.

The socioeconomic profile of a typical visitor could be deduced from the following figures: 62% of interviewed visitors were male; 56% had university studies, 30% had secondary studies and 8% compulsory schooling; 46% are between 31 and 49 years old, 27% between 18 and 30 and 27% are older than 49 years old; 30% stated to have a level of income between 1000 and 1500 euros per month, 19% between 1000 and 1500 euros per month, 16% stated to have no income; 13% revealed to have a level of income greater than 2000 euros per month and 5% rejected to answer this question. Most of interviewed visitors stated to have an employment and 13% said to be unemployed.

Once sample characteristics have been commented, the econometric results are presented below. The Poisson model estimated in this paper has the following form:

$$\ln(\lambda_i) = \gamma_0 + \beta\text{Cost}_i + \gamma_1\text{Income}_i + \gamma_2\text{Age}_i + \gamma_3\text{Sex}_i \qquad (4)$$

where Cost_i is the travel cost.[1] A reference cost of 0.19 euros per kilometre has been used to translate to euros the distance covered. When an interviewed person travelled in group in the same private vehicle, the cost of the travel assigned was total expense of the travel divided by the people in the group; Income$_i$ is the income per month of the visitor. Interviewed person was asked to choose one of five income intervals and the average of the interval chosen was assigned. Age$_i$ and Sex$_i$ were the age and sex of the interviewee.

Regression results are shown in the following Table 1:

We observe cost variable has a negative sign; the greater the travel cost is, the lower the number of visits made. Income variable also shows a negative sign. So, the greater the income of the visitor is, the smaller the number of visits made. So, visits to the park would be an inferior good. So, it could be inferred that the greater the income of a visitor is the smaller is the number of visits to this place since another leisure places and options would be available. Age has a positive sign; so, older people tend to visit the park more frequently. Sex variable (taking into account the way in which it was codified as a dichotomous one) has a positive sign, indicating that men visit more this area than women.

Taking $-1/\beta$ as consumer surplus associated to one visit, we obtain a consumer surplus for a visit of 5.09 euros. This is the benefit of the use of the El Valle and Carrascoy Natural Park as a recreational place for a visit of one person that uses to last one morning or one afternoon. It can be considered a conservative value since other concepts of cost, as time cost opportunity, have not been included, and this method is sensitive to costs used. It can be also considered a realistic figure since it is quite acceptable as the expected benefit that a person could obtain from a visit lasting some hours. Conceptually, in this case, the consumer surplus is the difference between the willingness to pay of one person for the visit and the cost incurred to make it. This result is comparable with Mangan et al. (2013) that estimated the recreational value of Pakistan's largest freshwater lake using individual travel cost method. They obtained a consumer surplus of US$ 14 (11.2 euros) per person per visit. Differences in the lasting of the visit, the level of income of visitors (this lake is visited by persons with medium-high level of income) and characteristics of the environmental goods, make logical differences in consumer surpluses. The results of the other two papers cited in this survey that use travel cost methods, Wallentin (2016), are not comparable to ours since methodology and research objectives are different.

We should remind that this is not the total value of the park but the recreational one since other non-use values are not measured by this method.

Conclusion and implications

El Valle and Carrascoy Natural Park is one of the most extensive protected natural areas in the Region of Murcia, Spain. Its proximity to the city of Murcia and other villages has turned this area into the most visited natural park by the inhabitants of the region and, potentially, this territory may suffer an important human impact. During last years, this natural park has acquired a recreational profile for the enjoyment of people together with a possible decline in its environmental quality and use. In this way, it has become necessary the implementation of protection policies that allowed a sustainable use of the park.

Nonetheless, in protected natural areas with high visitation, tourism and conservation can combine for a sustainable symbiotic relationship where tourism helped to maintain ecosystems since a part of visitors' expenditures can be destined to nature protection.

Table 1. Estimate of model [4].

Variable	Coefficient	Std. Error	z-Statistic	Prob
C	2.716013	0.099666	27.25114	0.0000
COST	−0.196335	0.011729	−16.73926	0.0000
INCOME	−0.000253	3.31E-05	−7.645440	0.0000
AGE	0.030568	0.001814	16.84845	0.0000
SEX	0.159705	0.050040	3.191546	0.0014

R-squared 0.570803
Adjusted R-squared 0.552142

This paper has put the first stone in this way, as a mean of helping the stakeholders to improve the management and protection of such natural asset by proving a valuation of one visit and a clear visitor profile. This is a useful information for decision-making and cost-benefit analysis.

The research has computed the recreational value of one visit of one person to the El Valle and Carrascoy Natural Park by relying on the individual travel cost method. Nonetheless, as this method allows us to value only recreational use, further work is needed to complete the picture of the environmental value of the park. Results obtained provide information on its recreational or tourist value to users and institutions in charge of its management. A consumer surplus or benefit of one visit (of one person) to this natural environment has been estimated in 5.09 euros. If total visitors figure was available, a total tourist valuation could be obtained, that had to be taken into account in the decision-making and policy design process that affected this area.

As people react to prices and the entrance to the park is free, we can deduce that an entrance fee would reduce the number of visitors and could be an instrument in case of overcrowding. Besides, in the case of public sector financial help scarcity, the revenue obtained in this way could support its sustainable management. Nonetheless, given that is a recreational and environmental good without closed substitutive places and that we could infer it is used by people with less leisure substitutive goods (we obtained a negative relation between level of income and number of visits) we could think an entrance fee was not socially advisable. It seems more acceptable to increment signalling and information about a proper use since these are also the major demands stated by visitors. Given data of total visitors and the value of a visit estimated in this paper, we could infer the level of public investment in recreational aspects of the park that is socially desirable.

The use of experiment choice could allow us to obtain other values of this area, as the environmental ones, and even valuations of different tourist activities. These would be possible future extensions of this research.

Note

1. There is no unanimity about the concepts to include in travel cost when applying the method. All the authors agree including oil expense and transport tickets. Nonetheless, there is no agreement about including other concepts as meal expenses or the time of the visit. In this survey, a reference cost of 0.19 euros per kilometre has been used to translate to euros the distance covered; this is the quantity paid by the Spanish Administration when a civil servant uses his own car in a work travel; this quantity is the compensation for fuel and wear resulting from usage of the car. The time of the travel was not included. Given the park proximity to several cities, many visitors go on foot. This implies a longer travel for people that go on foot. When valuing the time of the travel, a paradox could emerge since people around the park could have a travel cost greater than people coming from more remote areas that came by car. That is why people coming on foot or by bicycle have been excluded in the estimate. The final sample used was of 98 visitors that came to the park by car.

Disclosure statement

No potential conflict of interest was reported by the authors.

References

Alcón-Provencio, F., Martínez-Paz, J. M., Contreras-López, S., & Navarro-Pay, N. (2015). *Caracterización y evaluación de preferencias de desarrollo de los principales espacios naturales del Grupo de Acción Local Campoder* [*Characterization and Evaluation of Preferences of Development of major natural areas of Local Action Group Campoder*]. Murcia: Ed. Campoder.

Araña, J. E., & León, C. J. (2016). Are tourists animal spirits? Evidence from a field experiment exploring the use of non-market based interventions advocating sustainable tourism. *Journal of Sustainable Tourism, 24*(3), 430–445.

Báez-Montenedro, A., Bedate Centeno, A., Sanz Lara, J. A., & Herrero Prieto, L. C. (2015). Contingent valuation and motivation analysis of tourist routes. Application to the cultural heritage of Valdivia (Chile). *Tourism Economics, 22*(3), 558–571.

Baral, N., Kaul, S., Heinen, J. T., & Ale, S. B. (2017). Estimating the value of the World Heritage Site designation: A case study from Sagarmatha (Mount Everest) National Park, Nepal. *Journal of Sustainable Tourism.* doi:10.1080/09669582.2017.1310866

Briassoulis, H. (2003). Crete: Endowed by nature, privileged by geography, threatened by tourism? *Journal of Sustainable Tourism, 11*(2–3), 97–115.

Brouwer, R., Turner, R. K., & Voisey, H. (2001). Public perception of overcrowding and management alternatives in a multi-purpose open access resource. *Journal of Sustainable Tourism, 9*(6), 471–490.

Butler, R. (1994). Seasonality in tourism: Issues and problems. In A. Seaton (Ed.), *Tourisms. The status of the art* (pp. 332–339). Chichester: Wiley.

Casey, J. F., Brown, C., & Schuhmann, P. (2010). Are tourists willing to pay additional fees to protect corals in Mexico? *Journal of Sustainable Tourism, 18*(4), 557–573.

Chiou, C. R., Lin, J. C., Liu, W. Y., & Lin, T. W. (2016). Assessing the recreational value of protective forests at Taitung Forest Park in Taiwan. *Tourism Economics, 22*(5), 1132–1140.

Choi, A. S., & Ritchie, B. W. (2014). Willingness to pay for flying carbon neutral in Australia: An exploratory study of offsetter profiles. *Journal of Sustainable Tourism, 22*(8), 1236–1256.

Cole, S. (2014). Tourism and water: From stakeholders to rights holders and what tourism businesses need to do. *Journal of Sustainable Tourism, 22*(1), 89–106.

Fleming, C. M., & Manning, M. (2015). Rationing access to protected natural areas: An Australian case study. *Tourism Economics, 21*(5), 995–1014.

Folmer, H., & Ierland, E. C. (1989). *Valuation methods and policy making in environmental economics.* Wageningen: H. Folmer E.C. van Ierland Editors.

Haab, C. H., & McConnell, K. (2002). *Valuing environmental and natural resources: The econometrics of non-market valuation.* Cheltenham: Edward Elgar.

Haneman, W. M. (1984). Welfare evaluations in contingent valuation experiment with discrete responses. *American Journal of Agricultural Economics, 63*(3), 332–341.

Hellerstein, N. D., & Mendelson, R. (1993). A theoretical foundation for Count Data Models. *American Journal of Agricultural Economics, 75*(3), 604–611.

Hergesell, A., & Dickinger, A. (2013). Environmentally friendly holiday transport mode choices among students: The role of price, time and convenience. *Journal of Sustainable Tourism, 21*(4), 596–613.

Kuvan, Y. (2010). Mass tourism development and deforestation in Turkey. *Anatolia: an International Journal of Tourism and Hospitality Research, 21*(1), 155–168.

Lai, I. K. W., & Hitchcock, M. (2017). Local reactions to mass tourism and community tourism development in Macau. *Journal of Sustainable Tourism, 25*(4), 451–470.

Lee, C. K., Lee, J. H., Kim, T. K., & Mjelde, J. W. (2010). Preferences and willingness to pay for bird-watching tour and interpretive services using a choice experiment. *Journal of Sustainable Tourism, 18*(5), 695–708.

Madrigal de Torres, J. (2015). Oficina de Impulso Socioeconómico del Medio Ambiente (OISMA). In *Memoria Anual de Gestión de 2015 Parque Regional El Valle y Carrascoy* [*2015 Annual Management Report of El Valle and Carrascoy Natutal Park*]. Murcia: Ed. CARM.

Mangan, T., Brouwer, R., Lohano, H. D., & Nangraj, G. M. (2013). Estimating the recreational value of Pakistan's largest freshwater lake to support sustainable tourism management using a travel cost model. *Journal of Sustainable Tourism, 21*(3), 473–486.

Mejía, C. V., & Sylvia Brandt, S. (2017). Utilizing environmental information and pricing strategies to reduce externalities of tourism: The case of invasive species in the Galapagos. *Journal of Sustainable Tourism, 25*(6), 763–778.

Moorhouse, T., D' Cruze, N. C., & Macdonald, D. W. (2017). Unethical use of wildlife in tourism: What's the problem, who is responsible, and what can be done? *Journal of Sustainable Tourism, 25*(4), 505–516.

Palmer, T., & Riera, A. (2003). Tourism and environmental taxes. With special reference to the "Balearic ecotax". *Tourism Management, 24*, 665–674.

Parsons, G. R. (2003). The travel cost model. In P. A. Champ, K. J. Boyle, & T. C. Brown (Eds.), *A primer on nonmarket valuation.* Dordrecht: Kluver.

Perman, R., Ma, Y., McGilvary, J., & Common, M. (2003). *Natural resources and environmental economics*. Harlow: Pearson Education.

Riera Font, A. (2000). Mass tourism and the demand for protected natural areas: A travel cost approach. *Journal of Environmental Economics and Management, 39*(1), 97–116.

Riera, P., García, D., Kriström, B., & Brännlund, R. (2005). *Manual de Economía Ambiental y de los Recursos Naturales [Environmental and Natural Resource Economics Handbook]*. Madrid: Ed. Thomson Paraninfo.

Saayman, M., & Saayman, A. (2017). Is the rhino worth saving? A sustainable tourism perspective. *Journal of Sustainable Tourism, 25*(2), 251–264.

Salam, M. A., Lindsay, G. R., & Beveridge, M. C. M. (2000). Eco-tourism to protect the Reserve Mangrove Forest the Sundarbans and its Flora and Fauna. *Anatolia: an International Journal of Tourism and Hospitality Research, 11*(1), 56–66.

Tisdell, C. (2004). *Nature-based tourism and the valuation of its environmental resources: Economic and other aspects* (Working paper 104). The University of Queensland, ISSN 1327-8231.

Wallentin, E. (2016). Choice of the angler. Estimating single-site recreation demand using revealed preference data. *Tourism Economics, 22*(6), 1338–1351.

Wuepper, D. (2016). What is the value of world heritage status for a German national park? A choice experiment from Jasmund, 1 year after inscription. *Tourism Economics, 23*(5), 1114–1123.

Synthetic indicators and sustainable coastal tourism in Murcia, Spain

María Belén Cobacho-Tornel

ABSTRACT

This paper proposes the use of synthetic indicators to measure the sustainability of tourist activity in the coastal tourist areas of the Region of Murcia, providing a comparative analysis. Based on indicators proposed by the World Tourism Organization, and using hypothetical targets provided by users, the results obtained have the advantage of being easily interpretable by policy-makers, showing the strengths and weaknesses of the coastal areas of the Region of Murcia with regards to tourist activity, related to sustainability in general, and to its different dimensions in particular, which makes it possible for policy-makers to focus on those aspects which require special attention. As far as we know, this is the first study quantifying sustainable tourist activity in the region.

Introduction

One of the most important economic activities in the Region of Murcia, situated on the south-east coast of Spain, is tourism, providing 11% of the regional GDP in 2016 (Comunidad Autónoma de la Región de Murcia [CARM], 2017). Tourist activity is highly concentrated along the coast of the region. The main coastal municipalities, representing 11.01% of the regional area, received almost 1,400,000 visitors in 2015 (Instituto de Turismo, 2016). The coast of the Region of Murcia enjoys good weather throughout the year, with warm temperatures and a large number of beaches. This is the main reason why this area has become an important tourist destination, receiving both national and European visitors, mainly from the United Kingdom, France and Germany (Murcia Turística, 2016).

Sun and beach tourism is the main type of tourism in the region, generating, in 2012, 80% of the income proceeding from tourist activities, followed by golf tourism (5%), and nautical tourism (4%) (Consejería de Turismo, Comercio y Consumo, 2004b). However, the high density of tourist visitors in these coastal areas, mainly during the holiday season, together with all the associated economic activities, entails an uneven distribution of tourist activity, resulting in important negative consequences, such as an alarming deterioration of local ecosystems and natural resources.

What measures are being taken to solve this problem? The *Master Plan for the Region of Murcia, 2006–2012* (Consejería de Turismo, Comercio y Consumo, 2004a) was presented with the aim of "strengthening the Region as an attractive, high-quality tourist destination, through sustainability-based strategies which combine economic profitability with the conservation of cultural, natural and historic heritage". The document reports the positive effects of tourism in the region, such as job creation, increase in income, and lower migration levels due to unemployment. On the other hand, the negative consequences include an increase in water, energy, and land consumption, forest fires, ecosystem disruption, and population flow towards tourist areas, among others.

The same document analyses the strengths and opportunities of sun and beach tourism in the region, as well as its weaknesses and threats. The main strengths include the large number of beaches, with two different seas along the same stretch of coast (the Mediterranean Sea and the *Mar Menor*), national and international recognition of several destinations, virgin beaches, protected areas, and high tourist accommodation availability. The weaknesses include high seasonality, an absence of cultural events outside of the summer months, the low environmental quality of some of the beaches, massive urban development, a lack of promenades, a lack of promotional material, transport and traffic problems, and drinking water restrictions, among others (Consejería de Turismo, Comercio y Consumo, 2004a).

In this context, sustainable tourism appears as an alternative form of tourism, with the aim of correcting, or alleviating, the negative effects of mass tourism. Sustainable tourism is defined by the World Tourism Organization (World Tourism Organization, [WTO], 2005) as "tourism that takes full account of its current and future economic, social and environmental impacts, addressing the needs of visitors, industry, the environment and host communities". It should be based on a few basic principles: (1) making optimal use of environmental resources which constitute a key element in tourism development; (2) respecting the socio-cultural authenticity of host communities; and (3) ensuring viable, long-term economic operations, providing socio-economic benefits to all stakeholders, and which are fairly distributed and which contribute towards alleviating poverty. Achieving this implies implementing tourist policies which guarantee the protection of those natural, social, cultural and economic resources which sustain tourist activity, providing a high level of tourist satisfaction, as well as respecting the current and future needs of the host community (Liu, 2003; Sharpley, 2000).

Literature review

In the Region of Murcia, both the Tourism Master Plan 2006–2012 (Consejería de Turismo, Comercio y Consumo, 2004a), and the Strategic Plan 2015–2019 (CARM, 2015) suggest establishing quality parameters for tourism and tourist infrastructure based on sustainability. In this sense, tourism management policies should be based on a measurement system of the sustainability of tourist activity. The WTO (2004) states that creating a system of indicators is an important step, not only in order to plan and manage tourist activity, but also to make and improve more sustainable decisions.

The importance of indicators as tools for facilitating the planning, managing and controlling of tourist destinations has been highlighted by Rebollo and Castiñeira (2010). The literature related to the use of indicators (whether aggregated in a composite indicator or not) in order to assess sustainability is ample. The information which these studies normally provide consists of sustainability rankings of different areas, showing those aspects which may be improved in these assessed areas in order to attain a higher position in the ranking (Blancas, Caballero, González, Lozano-Oyola, & Pérez, 2010b; Blancas, Lozano-Oyola, González, & Caballero, 2016; Miller, 2001; Rio & Nunes, 2012).

In order to achieve this aim while following the three aforementioned basic principles, the WTO (2004) suggests a list of indicators, classified into three different dimensions: social, economic and environmental. The social dimension covers all those measurements which quantify the social and cultural impacts of tourism on the host community. The economic dimension collects measurements in order to analyse a long-term feasibility of tourist activity from an economic point of view. Finally, the environmental dimension covers all those aspects related to the conservation and protection of natural resources and ecosystems.

For proper decision-making in tourist activity management, allowing the strengthening of weak points while minimizing negative impacts, it is crucial that policy-makers have access to tools which can help them to evaluate the sustainable nature of tourist activity, and hence allow them to define actions which will improve the sustainability level.

The aim of this paper is to conduct a comparative analysis, from a quantitative point of view, of sustainable tourism in the main coastal destinations of the Region of Murcia. With this aim in mind, information about sustainable tourism at the municipality level in the region was collected, and the Goal Programming Synthetic Indicator proposed by Blancas et al. (2010b) was adapted to the singularities of the coastal tourist destinations of the region, in order to rank the municipalities according to their levels of sustainability.

The calculated synthetic indicator shows the relative situation of the tourist destinations regarding sustainability, providing a useful tool not only for planning and managing tourism, but also for promoting more sustainable policies in these destinations. This method allows us to know which areas are more or less environmentally friendly, while at the same time maintaining economic profitability, employment, poverty reduction and social needs.

This is the first work dealing with the sustainability of tourist activity in the Region of Murcia from a quantitative point of view. This paper presents important and concrete (quantitative) information about the sustainability of coastal tourist activity in the Region of Murcia, providing an important tool for tourism decision makers, managers and businesses for presenting the destinations in the Region as attractive and competitive. New stability analyses were provided, varying not only aspiration levels (Blancas et al., 2010b; Blancas, González, Guerrero, & Lozano, 2010a), but also carrying out stability analysis at four different levels: aspiration levels, strengths and weaknesses, dimensions, and indicators. This makes it possible to establish a highly stable pattern in the ranking of destinations.

Methodology

The Goal Programming Synthetic Indicator proposed by Blancas et al. (2010b) and which draws on the work of Diaz-Balteiro and Romero (2004) for the analysis of sustainable tourism, calculates a composite measure synthesizing the strengths of an area regarding a series of goals proposed for each sustainability measure, and also the weaknesses presented by that area with regards to these goals, allowing compensations between strengths and weaknesses in a final overall measurement. It is called the Goal Programming Indicator because it follows the concept of *goal* in the sense defined by that branch of Multi-Objective Optimization. (Charnes & Cooper, 1961). Goal Programming is a linear programming method used in decision-making situations with multiple objectives, and which aims to find the nearest solution to a set of goals established by an expert panel. The sustainable tourism synthetic indicator does not use linear programming, but it does use the same concept of goal.

This method classifies the available indicators as *positive* when a greater value of the indicator is considered to be better, or *negative*, when a lower value of the indicator is considered to be better. The *aspiration levels* or goals for any indicator must first be established. An aspiration level is the value of an indicator which is considered to be the desired level for that measurement. Aspiration levels should be proposed by expert decision-makers. When this is not possible, values proportional to the average value of the indicator can be used (Blancas et al., 2010a): $N_j^+ = \alpha \cdot \bar{I}_j^+$ (with $\alpha > 0$) when I_j^+ is a positive indicator, or $N_k^- = \beta \cdot \bar{I}_k^-$, (with $\beta > 0$), when I_k^- is a negative indicator. Once the aspiration levels have been determined, a goal for each area and indicator is established, introducing new variables which quantify the distance of the indicator value from the aspiration level:

$$I_i + n_i - p_i = N_I \tag{1}$$

where I_i is the value of the indicator I measured in the area $i = 1, 2, \ldots, n$; N_I is the aspiration level established for the indicator I; and n_i, p_i are the deviation variables of the area i, calculated as follows:

$$n_i = \begin{cases} N_I - I_i & \text{if } I_i < N_I \\ 0 & \text{otherwise} \end{cases} \quad p_i = \begin{cases} I_i - N_I & \text{if } I_i > N_I \\ 0 & \text{otherwise} \end{cases} \tag{2}$$

Deviation variables are non-negative, and at least one of them will be zero ($n_i \cdot p_i = 0$). If the value of a positive indicator in an area is higher than the aspiration level, it is understood that there is an achievement or fulfilment of that area in that dimension, and the distance from the indicator value to the aspiration level counts as a strength. On the other hand, if the value is below the aspiration level (non-fulfilment), it is considered a weakness. The opposite occurs with negative indicators. For this reason, the variable which is desired to have a non-zero value is the positive deviation variable in the case of a positive indicator, and the variable which is desired to have a non-zero value is the negative deviation variable in the case of a negative indicator.

Once the goals are established and the deviation variables calculated, the Net Goal Programming Synthetic Indicator, GPI_i, is the weighted sum of all the strengths or fulfilment levels (ratios of the desired variables over the aspiration levels) minus the weighted sum of all the weaknesses (ratios of the undesired variables over the aspiration levels):

$$GPI_i = w^+ \left[\sum_{j \in J} \frac{w_j p_{ij}^+}{N_j^+} + \sum_{k \in K} \frac{w_k n_{ik}^+}{N_k^-} \right] - w^- \left[\sum_{j \in J} \frac{w_j n_{ij}^+}{N_j^+} + \sum_{k \in K} \frac{w_k p_{ik}^+}{N_k^-} \right] \tag{3}$$

J indicates the number of positive indicators, w_j the weight assigned to the indicator j or the relative importance given to it with respect to the other indicators, p_{ij}^+ the positive deviation variable of the indicator j measured in the area i, N_j^+ the aspiration level of the positive indicator j, K is the number of negative indicators, w_k the weight assigned to the k indicator, n_{ik}^- the negative deviation variable of the k indicator measured in area i, and N_k^- the aspiration level of the negative indicator k. Finally, we introduced into this work the possibility of establishing different weights to the strength and weakness measurements. These weights are w^+ and w^-, respectively.

This synthetic indicator allows us to compare the achievements in sustainable tourism of an area with respect to other areas with similar characteristics, both as a global measurement of sustainable tourism, and also according to the dimensions of sustainable tourism. Stability analysis should be carried out in order to check how the results vary when different parameters are considered.

The WTO (2004) published a guide promoting the use of sustainable tourism indicators as instruments to be used by business managers and policy-makers for process planning and management at tourist destinations. In order to define a system of indicators for evaluating the sustainability of the destinations, we used the WTO (2004) guidelines to identify sustainable objectives in the coastal destinations of the region. We also completed the list of indicators with others proposed in local studies (Blancas et al., 2010b; Sancho & García, 2006), as well as with several indicators added ad hoc as approaches for others that were not available. The final list of indicators used was unavoidably determined by the availability of statistics at the municipality level. The municipalities considered were the main sun and beach tourism destinations of the region, namely *Águilas, Los Alcázares, Cartagena, Mazarrón, San Javier* and *San Pedro del Pinatar*.

Águilas, in the south-west of the Region, is a municipality with around 34,800 inhabitants (2015). It has 35 beaches and 28 km of coast along the Mediterranean Sea (Región de Murcia Digital web). *Los Alcázares* has 15,605 inhabitants and is located in the east of the region, with the Mar Menor to the east. Its economy has changed from mainly agricultural and fishing activities to an important development of the service sector due to the tourism boom of the last few decades. *Cartagena*, with 216,300 inhabitants, is the second largest municipality in the region. The Mediterranean Sea lies to the south of the city, and the Mar Menor to the east. The surrounding area is rich and diverse in wildlife despite intensive mining, industrial and tourist activity throughout its history. In recent years, tourist activity in Cartagena has increased significantly due to its importance as a cruise destination and the restoration of its cultural and historical heritage. *Mazarrón* is a municipality which lies on the Mediterranean Sea and which has 32,150 inhabitants. It has 35 km of coast with beaches, cliffs and small coves, some of which are in a state of almost virgin conservation. Its main economic activity has changed over the last century from mining to tourism, agriculture, and fishing. *San Javier* is a municipality with around 31,900 inhabitants and lies on both the Mediterranean and the Mar Menor seas. It has an airport and an important cultural offering. Finally, *San Pedro del Pinatar* has around 24,340 inhabitants and also lies on both seas. The nearby regional park is an important wetland area of salt flats, beaches and dunes.

Despite there being a great deal of information about tourism in the Region, statistics at the municipality level are scarce, incomplete and non-systematic. We finally obtained information about 51 indicators, 26 of which correspond to the social dimension, 15 to the economic dimension and 10 to the environmental dimension. The year considered was 2015 (the latest with available information at the time this study was conducted), or the nearest year possible when information for 2015 was not available and little variation could be expected. It was necessary to consult a long list of sources proceeding from different institutions. We also sent emails to city councils requesting information, obtained data from tourism websites, and quantified qualitative information. The same source was considered whenever possible, in order to avoid differences in the measurement methods.

Table 2 (Appendix) presents a complete list of indicators belonging to the social, economic and environmental dimensions respectively, indicating the key aspect of sustainability to be evaluated, the question to be analysed, the indicator, and its direction of improvement (positive or negative). When the figures of the indicators are observed, they show variations among the different municipalities, and none of the municipalities presents either the best or the worst value in a majority of the indicators, so that no predictable ranking of municipalities in sustainability exists.

Results

One of the advantages of this method is that the initial data does not need to be normalized in order to calculate the composite indicator. This is an advantage when it comes to interpreting the results, which is different to other methodologies, such as the one based on Principal Component Analysis proposed by Blancas et al. (2010a), or the PROMETHEE method used by Blancas et al. (2006).

In the first stage, we compute the synthetic indicator for each dimension: social, economic and environmental, which simplifies the process and allows us to observe sustainability by dimension, without considering simultaneously all the information included in the system. In the second stage, we obtain the global aggregated indicator, which provides a multi-dimensional measurement of sustainability.

In order to obtain these synthetic indicators, the first step is to establish aspiration levels for each indicator. When a panel of experts is not available, values proportional to the average of each indicator are calculated. In the general case, following the study of Blancas et al. (2010a), aspiration levels were fixed at $\alpha = 1.25$ times the average value of the indicator for positive indicators, and $\beta = 0.8$ times the average value of the indicator for negative ones. With these (rather demanding) goals, the most general case was considered, using the same weights for strengths and weaknesses ($w^+ = w^- = 0.5$ in expression (3)).

Table 1 shows the results of the Goal Programming Synthetic Indicator (GPI), by dimension (social, economic and environmental) and the rankings for this general case. The last block in the table presents the results for the global synthetic indicator and the global ranking. All the municipalities "fail" in sustainability: the global composite indicator GPI is negative for all the municipalities, which means that all the municipalities present a higher overall value for weaknesses than for strengths. In other words, the sum of the ratios of the desirable or "good" distances

Table 1. Synthetic goal programming indicator, by dimension and with overall results. general case (equal weights for all the elements).

MUNICIPALITIES	Social dim.		Economic dim.		Environm. dim.		Global dim.			
	GPIs	Ranking	GPIe	Ranking	GPIev	Ranking	GPI⁺	GPI⁻	GPI	Ranking
Águilas	−0,097	2	−0,265	6	0,006	1	0,085	0,322	−0,119	3
Los Alcázares	−0,178	6	−0,037	2	−0,314	6	0,098	0,451	−0,177	6
Cartagena	0,046	1	−0,074	3	−0,022	3	0,180	0,213	−0,016	1
Mazarrón	−0,151	5	−0,194	5	−0,100	4	0,076	0,372	−0,148	5
San Javier	−0,125	3	0,038	1	−0,020	2	0,150	0,222	−0,036	2
San Pedro P.	−0,141	4	−0,089	4	−0,136	5	0,095	0,338	−0,122	4

Source: Author.

lies below the sum of the non-desirable or "bad" ones. In this scenario, Cartagena presents the best (or rather the least bad) performance in terms of global sustainability, followed by San Javier, Águilas, San Pedro del Pinatar, Mazarrón and finally Los Alcázares. However, the differences in these net values are not large, which could suggest possible changes when the parameters are varied. In this sense, different scenarios are presented in the stability analysis subsection.

Analysing the results by dimension can shed some light on the reasons why these results were obtained. Figure 1 shows the rankings obtained by each municipality by dimension. No municipality obtains either the highest GPI for all three dimensions, or the lowest value. Los Alcázares gets the lowest GPI in both the environmental and the social dimension. San Javier and Cartagena lie in the top three positions in all three dimensions.

When we analyse the situation of the tourist destinations in the highest positions, we find that, in the social dimension, the top two municipalities (Cartagena and Águilas) present very low population variation (under 0.5%), and also low levels of available income variation (under 1%). Pressure on the local culture measured in terms of foreign population is low, with percentages of foreign population under 13%. Expenditure per capita on public transport is high compared with that of the municipalities in the bottom positions. The main weaknesses in these municipalities are the lack of sanitary facilities on the beaches, low public spending on mobility, and public safety. Regarding the economic dimension, the municipalities in the top positions have at least 20% high-quality tourist accommodation, a large number of restaurants, high public spending on the promotion of tourism, and an easily accessible nearby airport. Their main weakness is unemployment, with an unemployment rate above 12%, similar to that of those in the bottom positions.

In the environmental dimension, those municipalities with higher public spending on the environment, and a lower consumption of drinking water stand out. From a global point of view, the best situation in terms of sustainability is found in those municipalities with higher public spending on public transport and on the environment, and with a greater availability of high-quality tourist accommodation. On the other hand, the worst levels of global sustainability are found in those municipalities with low spending on public transport, a lower level of available tourist accommodation (more specifically, high-quality tourist accommodation), low public spending on tourist information and the promotion of tourism, and high water consumption.

Observing the information by municipality, the main strength of the municipality of Cartagena lies on the social dimension, despite its being the only municipality which presents a positive net social indicator (Table 1). On the economic and environmental dimensions, Cartagena occupies the third position (Figure 1). The best value on the economic dimension is that of San Javier, being the only municipality with a net positive indicator on that dimension (Table 1). Finally, Águilas shows the best performance on the environmental dimension, with a slightly positive net indicator, close to zero. On the other hand, Los Alcázares lies in second place on the economic dimension, but is the worst on both the social and environmental dimensions. Mazarrón and San Pedro move between the fourth and fifth positions, depending on the dimension.

Table 2. Sustainable tourism indicators of the social, economic and environmental dimensions.

Baseline aspects	Sustainability issues	Indicator	Sign
Sustainable tourism indicators of the social dimension			
Social and cultural effects on host community	Health services	No. of health centres/10,000 inhabitants	+
	Transport services and support	No. of passenger transportation permissions/ 10,000 inhabitants	+
		Public spending (€) per capita on public transport	+
	Financial services	No. of bank offices/10,000 inhabitants	+
	Pharmacy services	No. of pharmacies/10,000 inhabitants	+
	Other services	No. of service establishments/10,000 inhabitants	+
	Public services on beaches	% beaches with public toilets	+
		% beaches with showers or taps	+
	Sports activities	Funds for sports facilities/resident	+
	Cultural facilities	No. of libraries/10,000 inhabitants	+
		No. of museums/10 km^2	+
	Cultural activities	No. of cultural activities/million (€) of total public spending	+
Local public safety and welfare	Public safety	Public spending (€) per capita on citizen safety and mobility	+
	Local welfare	Public spending (€) per capita on community welfare	+
Preservation of cultural heritage	Protection of cultural traditions	No. of popular celebrations declared of tourist interest	+
		Spending (€) per capita on protection and management of historical and artistic heritage	+
		Spending (€) per capita on popular festivals	+
Effects on local population structure	Stability of population level	% variation in the population (absolute value)	-
		Migratory balance (abs. value)/ 10,000 inhabitants	-
		Natural increase rate (absolute value)	-
	Increase of young population	% population younger than 35	+
	Population ageing	% non-working population older than 55	-
	Population density	Population density per area unit (km^2)	-
Social burden on destination	Imposition of foreign culture (pressure over the local culture)	% foreign population	-
Effects on population welfare	Effects on disposable income	Disposable income variation	+
	Effects on access to housing	Cadastral value (€)/Resident	-
Sustainable tourism indicators of the economic dimension			
Economic benefit for local community	Tourist demand volume	No. services rendered in tourism offices (2nd quarter)	+
	Investment in property	Cadastral value per urban unit	+
	Employment generated for service sector	Proportion of contracts in service sector	+
	Unemployment in destination	Unemployment rate per population from 15 to 65 years old	-
	Telephone communications	No. phone lines/1,000 inhabitants	+
	Internet communications	No. Internet lines (only Movistar broadband)/1,000 inhabitants	+
Diverse experiences supply	Tourist accommodation availability	No. accommodation places/100 visitors to tourist offices	+
	Quality of tourist accommodation	No. high-class accommodation places/100 visitors to tourist offices	+
	Restaurant availability	No. restaurant places/100 inhabitants	+
	Tourist experience promotion	No. tourist information offices	+
		Existence of tourism website	+
		Public spending (€) per capita on tourism promotion	+
	Active tourism availability	No. active tourism businesses/10,000 inhabitants	+
Tourism-related transport	Access to airports	Time (minutes) to nearest airport	-
Sustainable tourism indicators of the environmental dimension			
Ecosystem protection	Natural resources protection	% beach area with "Blue Flag" distinction	+
		% beach area with "Q for Quality" distinction	+
		Public spending (€) per capita on environment	+
	Forest degradation	% forest area affected by fires	-
Coastal marine water quality		Quality of bathing water	+

(Continued)

Table 2. (Continued).

Baseline aspects	Sustainability issues	Indicator	Sign
Intensity of use	Area for agricultural activities	% cultivated agricultural area	+
	Drinking water consumption	Drinking water consumption (m^3/inhabitant per year)	-
Pollution	Vehicles density	No. vehicles/driver	-
Waste management	Solid waste treatment and management	Public spending (€) per capita on waste treatment and management	+
		No. eco-parks/10,000 inhabitants	+

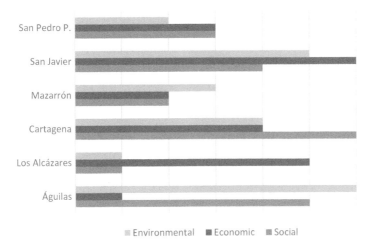

Figure 1. Ranking in the synthetic indicator by dimension.

The longest bar indicates the first position.

Source: Author.

Stability analysis

Different parameters in the system were varied in order to observe possible changes in the results. In the general case, negative net GPI were obtained for all the municipalities, which suggests that the aspiration levels were, maybe, too ambitious. Figure 2 shows some results of the sensibility analysis.

Figure 2(a) shows the ranking obtained when α varies in the interval [0.9,1.35] and β remains constant. When α>1, horizontal lines for all the municipalities show that there is no change in the global ranking if the aspiration level for positive indicators is too demanding (i.e. above the average value). We also tried using lower values for α (that is, aspiration levels equal to or less than the average). In this case, there are variations among positions 3–6, but the first two positions remain the same.

Something similar occurs when β varies in the interval [0.65,1.1] while maintaining α fixed at the 1.25 level. Cartagena and San Javier maintain the first and second positions respectively, and little variation is found in the rest of the positions, except for when the aspiration level for the negative indicators equals or exceeds the average.

The global GPI when α varies in the interval [0.9,1.35] is greater for less demanding aspiration levels. In other words, it is a decreasing function dependent on α. Only two of the municipalities, Cartagena and San Javier, obtain positive net values in the lower half of the interval. The values of the net GPI are quite similar for the municipalities of Águilas and San Pedro along the whole interval.

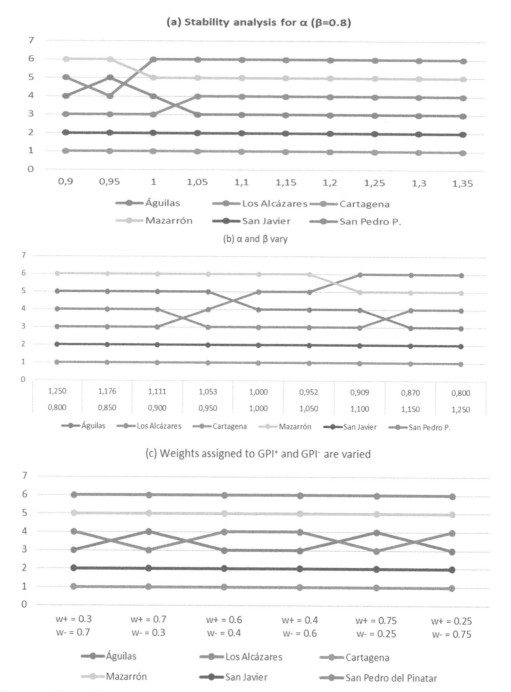

Figure 2. Stability analysis.

Source: Author.

When both positive and negative indicators are assigned variable aspiration levels, some variation in the ranking appears (Figure 2(b)). Cartagena and San Javier remain in the first and second positions in the ranking, respectively. Los Alcázares drops from third to last position as the aspiration levels become more demanding. San Pedro del Pinatar alternates between positions 3 and 4, Águilas moves up from position 5 to position 3, and Mazarrón from position 6 to position 5. The graph shows a stable pattern for positions 1 and 2.

Then the weights assigned to strengths and weaknesses, (which were equal in the general case) were varied (Figure 2(c)). This did not affect either the top two positions (Cartagena and San Javier) or the bottom two (Mazarrón and Los Alcázares), but the central positions varied between Águilas and San Pedro del Pinatar. This is not surprising, as these two municipalities present quite similar GPI.

When weights between dimensions are varied, some small changes appear. Cartagena loses top place in favour of San Javier if the social dimension is given little importance and the economic dimension is allocated greater weight than the environmental one. Los Alcázares remains in the last position except for the case when the economic importance is assigned double the weight of the other two dimensions, as this municipality achieved the second-best position on the economic dimension.

Finally, the weights assigned to the initial indicators were also varied. A deterministic situation was first considered, giving double importance to those indicators that could depend on policy-makers to some extent (as, for example, the amount of hotel accommodation available), compared to the importance given to other indicators which do not directly depend on policy-makers (such as, for example, population density, or the number of visitors). In this case, the six municipalities analysed maintain a negative global GPI, but Cartagena drops to second position in favour of San Javier, which moves up to the top position, as a consequence of Cartagena's worse economic performance. Águilas and San Pedro del Pinatar exchange third and fourth positions, and Mazarrón and Los Alcázares maintain the fifth and sixth positions, respectively. After 100 trials, randomly assigning weights to the 51 initial indicators, Cartagena showed the best global performance in sustainability in 73% of the trials, followed by San Javier, which came top in the remaining 23% of the cases. The lowest overall measurement in sustainability was presented by Los Alcázares in 66% of the cases, and Mazarrón in 30%.

Conclusion and implications

In this study, information about 51 indicators for sustainable tourism in the main coastal municipalities of the Region of Murcia was collected, in order to calculate a composite, multi-dimensional measurement quantifying the level of fulfilment and non-fulfilment of each assessed unit, compared to the others, with regards to a series of target levels of sustainable tourism.

With aspiration levels above the average for positive indicators, and below the average for negative indicators, and assigning the same importance to all the elements in the system (indicators, dimensions, and strengths and weaknesses measurements), the six municipalities analysed present a negative value for the overall net indicator. This shows that the level of non-fulfilment is greater than the measurement of fulfilment for all the municipalities studied.

The municipality of Cartagena presents the highest value in the overall composite indicator, closely followed by the municipalities of San Javier, then Águilas, San Pedro del Pinatar, Mazarrón and, finally, Los Alcázares, although the distances between their respective values are not large. This ranking is found in around 20% of the situations analysed. In general, positions 1 and 2, occupied by Cartagena and San Javier, are quite stable. They stand out in terms of higher public spending on public transport and on the environment, and with a higher availability of high-quality tourist accommodation. On the other hand, the dimensional indicators show several factors which need to be addressed in those destinations with a lower overall score. These include improving public transport, increasing the amount of tourist accommodation, especially high-quality accommodation, increasing public spending on tourist information and the promotion of tourism, and regulation in order to reduce levels of water consumption.

Having highlighted the strengths and weaknesses of the main tourist destinations in the region with respect to sustainable tourism, this study provides a starting point for policy-makers to address the requirements for improving the sustainable nature of tourist activity. It would be necessary to introduce important improvements in this field in the future. The indicator system applied is not exempt of significant deficiencies. The lack of information at the municipal level in the region suggests that the approach taken does not include many of the important indicators proposed by the World Tourism Organization in order to assess sustainability. Thus, the main implication of this study is that statistical data needs to be collected periodically and systematically by reliable official sources. This would improve our knowledge not only of the relative performance of tourist destinations with respect to their neighbouring destinations (or competitors), but also of the evolution of their sustainability with respect to one another over a longer period of time, in this way allowing them to adjust to a process of change towards a more sustainable kind of tourism.

Disclosure statement

No potential conflict of interest was reported by the author.

References

Blancas, F. J., Caballero, R., González, M., Guerrero, F. M., Lozano-Oyola, M., Molina, J., & Rodríguez, B. (2006). Análisis del turismo de las costas andaluzas bajo un enfoque multicriterio [Analysis of tourism in the Andalusian coast using a multicriteria approach]. *XIV Jornadas de Asepuma y II Encuentro Internacional.* Retrieved from https://goo.gl/aamYpu

Blancas, F. J., Caballero, R., González, M., Lozano-Oyola, M., & Pérez, F. (2010b). Goal programming synthetic indicators: An application for sustainable tourism in Andalusian coastal counties. *Ecological Economics, 69,* 2158–2172.

Blancas, F. J., González, M., Guerrero, F., & Lozano, M. (2010a). Indicadores sintéticos de turismo sostenible: Una aplicación para los destinos turísticos de andalucía [synthetic indicators for sustainable tourism. A study for touristic destinations in Andalusia. *Revista Electrónica de Comunicaciones y Trabajos de ASEPUMA, 11,* 85–118. Retrieved from http://www.revistarecta.com/n11/recta_11_09.pdf

Blancas, F. J., Lozano-Oyola, M., González, M., & Caballero, R. (2016). Sustainable tourism composite indicators: A dynamic evaluation to manage changes in sustainability. *Journal of Sustainable Tourism, 24*(10), 1403–1424.

CARM Comunidad Autónoma de la Región de Murcia (2015). Plan Estratégico 2015–2019 [strategic plan 2015–2019]. Retrieved October, 2017, from https://goo.gl/7Hqnq6

CARM Comunidad Autónoma de la Región de Murcia (2017). Balance Turístico de la Región de Murcia, 2016 [analysis of tourism in the region of Murcia, 2016]. Retrieved September, 2017, from https://goo.gl/J1ngCy

Charnes, A., & Cooper, W. (1961). *Management models and industrial applications of linear programming.* New York: John Wiley.

Consejería de Turismo, Comercio y Consumo (2004a). Plan director de turismo de la región de Murcia 2006–2012 [director plan for tourism in the region of Murcia 2006–2012]. Retrieved October, 2017, from http://goo.gl/t9v5fq

Consejería de Turismo, Comercio y Consumo (2004b). Definición del modelo turístico de la región de Murcia (2006–2012) [definition of the touristic model in the region of Murcia]. Retrieved August, 2017, from http://www.carm.es/ctyc/institucional/turismo/2.2801.pdf

Diaz-Balteiro, L., & Romero, C. (2004). Sustainability of forest management plans: A discrete goal programming approach. *Journal of Environmental Management, 71,* 351–359.

Instituto de Turismo (2016). Datos de la actividad turística en la región de Murcia: Año 2015 [data of touristic activity in the region of Murcia, 2015]. Retrieved 12 September, 2017, from https://goo.gl/5ebw12

Liu, Z. (2003). Sustainable tourism development: A critique. *Journal of Sustainable Tourism, 11*(6), 459–475.

Miller, G. (2001). The development of indicators for sustainable tourism: Results of a Delphi survey of tourism researchers. *Tourism Management, 22*(4), 351–362.

Rebollo, J. F., & Castiñeira, C. J. (2010). Renovación y reestructuración de los destinos turísticos consolidados del litoral: Las prácticas recreativas en la evolución del espacio turístico [Remodelling tourism coastal destinations: Recreational activities in the touristic destinations evolution]. *Boletín de la Asociación de Geógrafos Españoles, 53,* 329–353.

Rio, D., & Nunes, L. M. (2012). Monitoring and evaluation tool for tourism destinations. *Tourism Management Perspectives, 4*, 64–66.

Sancho, A., & García, G. (2006). ¿Qué indica un indicador? Análisis comparativo en los destinos turísticos [what does an indicator indicate? comparative analysis in touristic destinations]. *Revista de Análisis Turístico, 2*, 69–85.

Sharpley, R. (2000). Tourism and sustainable development: Exploring the theoretical divide. *Journal of Sustainable Tourism, 8*(1), 1–19.

Turística, M., (2016). Sol y Playa. Sun and Beach. Retrieved 10, August 2017, from https://www.murciaturistica.es/es/sol_y_playa/

World Tourism Organization, WTO. (2004). *Indicators of sustainable development for tourism destinations: A guidebook*. Madrid: Author.

World Tourism Organization, WTO (2005). Making tourism more sustainable - a guide for policy makers, 11–12. Retrieved 11 October, 2017, from http://sdt.unwto.org/content/about-us-5

Estimating the impact of cruise tourism through regional input–output tables

Andrés Artal-Tur (iD), José Miguel Navarro-Azorín (iD) and José María Ramos-Parreño (iD)

ABSTRACT

In this paper we estimate the economic impact of cruise tourism with an application to the Port of Cartagena, Spain. As a novelty, we build on a newly available regional input–output (IO) framework. This allows us to compute the indirect and induced effects of cruise ship visits, which adds to the direct effects obtained from survey data. Results identify the total impact in terms of employment, wages, gross operating surplus and value added. Methodologically, the use of regional IO tables improves the accuracy of previous methodologies building on country IO Tables. Results of the investigation provide important policy recommendations to the public and private stakeholders in order to manage this rising activity.

Introduction

Global cruise tourism has increased by an average annual rate of 4.2% over the last decade, increasing from 17.8 million passengers in 2009 to 24.7 million passengers in 2016 (Cruise Lines International Association [CLIA], 2017). Despite the more established tradition of this type of tourism in the North American market, the European continent has registered a remarkable upsurge in recent years, with a 200% increase in the number of passengers in the period 2001–2013. Within Europe, the Mediterranean ports and cities have emerged as the preferred destinations for cruise ships and visitors, with Spain, Italy, Greece and France leading the ranking. Understanding and quantifying the impact of cruise activity on tourism destinations is currently an important line of research. This has become a key issue both for public managers and for economic agents involved in this activity.

With regard to the recent growth of the cruise industry, North America holds the largest market share, with 12.2 million cruise passengers in the year 2014, followed by Europe with 6.4 million, out of a global total of 22 million cruise passengers. However, between 2001 and 2013 the number of passengers from Europe and from other parts of the world has also increased. International demand for cruises tripled for European passengers in the period 2001–2014. These cruises visited ports in the Mediterranean, the Baltic and other European regions, generating 29 million passenger visits at a total of around 250 European port cities (CLIA, 2015).

In the ranking of European ports, the Mediterranean countries again emerge as the most predominant, with nearly 15 million passengers in 2013 compared with 7 million passengers in Northern European ports. The ranking of ports of call by number of visits again shows the importance of the main Mediterranean tourist destinations (Italy, Spain, Greece, and France) within the European market. Spain is the second most popular cruise destination in Europe, after

Italy, with 4.9 million cruise passengers in 2013, which accounts for 16.9% of the European market. In Northern Europe, countries such as Norway, the UK, Sweden and Estonia are at the top of the ranking, but still lag quite far behind the Mediterranean destinations. In the case of cruise passengers to Spanish ports (embarkation, disembarkation and port of call passengers) between 2005 and 2016, numbers more than double during this period, leading to a total of 8.7 million passengers (CLIA, 2015).

The Annual Reports of the Spanish Port Authorities show the importance of the following ports in the national cruise market based on the total number of passengers: Barcelona, the Balearic Islands (Palma de Mallorca, Mahón and Ibiza), the Canary Islands (Santa Cruz, Las Palmas de Gran Canaria, Arrecife), Malaga, Cadiz, Valencia, Alicante, Cartagena, Vigo, La Coruña and Bilbao. Annual traffic data between 2005 and 2013 shows that Barcelona and the Balearic Islands are the leading Spanish Mediterranean ports, and that Tenerife and Las Palmas, in the Canary Islands, are the leading Spanish Atlantic ports. During the analysis period, we can see a significant increase in the number of cruise passengers to the ports of Barcelona, Valencia, Cadiz, Cartagena, Coruña, and Bilbao (Table 1). Regarding passenger traffic in the Port of Cartagena, the increase in the number of cruisers in recent years has been remarkable; despite a slight decrease in 2011 and 2012, there was a 39.6% increase between 2013 and 2016.

The Port of Cartagena in Spain is currently embarked on a process of growth and consolidation as a cruise ship destination. The main advantages of the Port of Cartagena as a cruise destination include its geographical location, which offers a natural refuge from adverse weather conditions for mooring ships, as well as its facilities, which include a 344 m mooring quay with a depth of 12 m, allowing the port to receive the largest of cruise ships. In 2012 the port was fitted with a new Cruise Terminal in the outer part of the Marina, near to the city centre and the cultural, leisure and commercial areas of the quay, which have the depth and manoeuvrability required for this type of vessels. The Port Authority of Cartagena plans to enlarge the cruise area in the near future, lengthening the mooring quay to 500 m and building a 5000 m^2 service area, at an estimated cost of 7.9 million euros.

Literature review

The original contribution of Dwyer and Forsyth (1998) established the structure for the computation of cruise-related expenditures, including those of passengers and operators (crew and vessel-related expenses). They also highlighted the limitations which result when estimating the regional impact of cruise visits, given the large amount of on-board spending by the same passengers. These authors claim that it is necessary to compute direct and overall effects of cruise ship visits at a national and regional level by using multiplier analysis, i.e. by using input–output (IO) methods. In their case study for Australia, they found that cruise tourism has a positive impact, and also

Table 1. Cruise passengers in Spanish ports 2003–2016 (thousands of passengers).

Autoridad Portuaria	2013	2016	Var (%)
Barcelona	2,599	2,687	3.39
Baleares	1,532	1,958	27.81
Las Palmas	830	1,105	33.13
Santa Cruz de Tenerife	794	884	11.34
Málaga	397	444	11.84
Valencia	473	403	−14.80
Bahía de Cádiz	375	385	2.67
Cartagena	134	187	39.55
Vigo	171	169	−1.17
A Coruña	156	126	−19.23
Alicante	41	89	117.07
Bilbao	56	86	53.57

Source: State Port Authority (2005-2016) (www.puertos.es), Ministry of Fomento (Spain).

highlighted several related costs. Further evidence includes several studies that encounter no significant impact for the case of Jamaica (Chase & McKee, 2003), and a positive impact for the southwest of England (Gibson & Bentley, 2006) and Belize (Quan-Novelo, Santoya, & Vellos, 2007). Other studies identify the differences in economic impact of being a home port in comparison with a port of call (Vina & Ford, 1998). Another branch of the literature focused on understanding the expenditure pattern of cruise tourists by running behavioural equations (Brida, Bukstein, Garrido, Tealde, & Zapata, 2010; Brida, Bukstein, & Tealde, 2012; Brida & Zapata, 2010a), and also on the socio-cultural and environmental impact of cruise tourism (Brida & Zapata, 2010b).

With regard to applications of IO analysis for cruise tourism, the most up-to-date and rigorous studies were carried out by BREA (2013) for the Port of Victoria (Canada) and the surrounding area, and by Worley and Akehurst (2013) for the economy of New Zealand. The study by BREA quantifies the direct spending of passengers and crew as well as vessel-related expenses using the survey method, and computes the direct and indirect economic impacts on the regional economy by employing the IO table of British Columbia. In the case of New Zealand, the authors present direct impact numbers for the 11 main ports of the country, building on data from port authorities and national accounts. They employ the IO framework of the economy of New Zealand in order to compute indirect and induced effects of cruise visits, while also applying non-survey methods to regionalize the national IO table for the analysis of individual ports.

The present study extends this line of research by estimating the regional economic impact of cruise tourism entering the Port of Cartagena. In doing so, we build on a newly available regional IO framework. This allows us to compute the indirect and induced effects of cruise ship visits, which add to the direct effects obtained from survey data. As a result, we identify the total impact of cruise visits in terms of the most important economic variables, i.e. employment, sales, wages and salaries, gross operating surplus and value added.

Methodology

Most studies analysing the impact of a Port Authority usually seek to quantify the capacity of a port for generating economic activity from its core business, namely freight transport. The economic impact is then captured by variables such as value added, employment, wage income, operating surplus and generated taxes. In addition, if one wishes to focus on the evaluation of the economic impact of the cruise industry associated with the port, the bulk of the effects stems from the activities related to the vessel and port operations (a common feature with freight transport), as well as from the expenditure of both the cruise passengers and crew. Subsequently, the general methodology of impact analysis usually employed has to be adapted in order to take this specific feature of cruise tourism into account.

The basic steps needed in the general analysis of the economic impact of port activities accounts for integrating three types of effects: direct, indirect and induced.

- The direct effect is the economic contribution (in terms of employment, value added, employee compensation, etc.) of the companies and public bodies associated with cruise tourism activity. The evaluation of the direct effect comes from data obtained from surveys and other primary sources of information (business databases, trade registers, etc.).
- The indirect effect measures the value of the purchases of goods and services made by cruise passengers and crew in the hinterland. It also includes the effects arising from the demand (purchases and investments) of port and dependent industries in relation to cruise tourism activity.
- The induced effect comprises the effects from private consumption by employed workers (as a result of the jobs created by the direct and indirect effects).

In the case of cruise tourism, the calculation of the direct effect is not conceptually very complex since it collects the activities of the port industry (Port Authority, consignee, etc.) during the visit of the ship to the city. However, the estimation of indirect and induced effects requires the formulation of several hypotheses and scenarios defining the intersectoral relationships between the cruise visit, the port industry and the other sectors of the regional economy. Several scenarios in this relationship would then lead to alternative methodological approaches found in the literature. In this study we opted to conduct the estimation of the indirect and induced effects by employing a rigorous IO framework. In particular, we have built on the analytical model and related information defined in the 2007 regional input–output table (R-IOT) for the Region of Murcia, where the Port of Cartagena is located.

The R-IOT employed in the study is part of the INTERTIO research project developed by the Lawrence Klein Institute/CEPREDE of the Universidad Autónoma of Madrid, Spain http://www.ceprede.es/index.asp (Llano, 1998, 2004). It develops a coherent framework of Regional-IOT for all 17 regions in Spain (EU NUTS-2 dimension) (INE, http://www.ine.es/daco/daco42/cne/meto dologiaio.pdf). The R-IOT 2007 for the Region of Murcia is a 35 × 35 symmetric table, including supply- and demand-side information for the whole regional economy, as well as all intersectoral relationships between the regional industries. A salient feature of this IO table is that it includes a convenient level of disaggregation for the transport activities since there is a breakdown for freight and transport activities as well as for land, rail, maritime and air transport services.

In the IO framework, the relationship between spending on purchases and investments of the port-dependent industries (the indirect impact vector, g), and the effective production necessary to satisfy this demand (the indirect effect, $y_{indirect}$) can be written as

$$y_{indirect} = \left(I - A^R\right)^{-1} g \tag{1}$$

where A^R is the matrix $n \times n$ of technical coefficients, whose characteristic element $\left\{a_{ij}^R\right\}$ measures the degree of use of intermediate consumption goods and services of *regional* origin produced by the branch of activity i for each unit of effective production of the branch j.

The matrix $\left(I - A^R\right)^{-1}$, known as the inverse Leontief matrix, plays a crucial role in the evaluation of the economic impact, as it allows us to calculate the effort in terms of production that each branch of activity must make in order to satisfy the demand formulated by the other branches, once all of the inter-industrial effects have been taken into account.

The rationale for Equation (1) is that companies buy inputs (e.g. transport material and fuel) from local suppliers; the production of these inputs generates additional output and employment in the local economy, given that the suppliers buy goods and services from other companies. Therefore, as a consequence of the successive rounds of local purchases, the global impact on the economy will be higher than that generated by the first round of expenditure. However, in each round the effect decreases. Equation (1) determines the effect of the initial purchases on local production by adding the effects generated in each of the aforementioned rounds. This is clear once we realize that the inverse Leontief matrix can be expressed as

$$\left(I - A^R\right)^{-1} = I + A^R + A^{R2} + A^{R3} + \dots, \tag{2}$$

where the first addition sign on the right captures the effect of purchases on production in the first round, the second addition sign represents the effect generated by the purchases in the second round, and so on.

A crucial consideration for estimating the indirect economic effect of port activities is the definition of the impact vector, g. This vector summarizes the information about purchases, general expenditures and investments made by port companies, as well as passenger and crew expenditure. The primary source of information is the data supplied by the companies themselves through surveys. When this information was not supplied, other available sources were used. In addition, in order to avoid double counting, the total internal operations of each of the analysed sectors (port and dependent industries) are deducted from the indirect impact vector, as they are already contained in the direct effect.

To calculate the indirect effect on variables other than gross production, we proceed as follows. Let us take, for example, added value as the economic variable of interest; in this case, we define an $n \times n$ diagonal matrix, denoted by D_{VA}, whose elements on the main diagonal are the gross value added per unit of gross production of each branch of activity. These coefficients are calculated by using the information provided by the R-IOT and are assumed to be constant. Then, by multiplying the indirect effect on production given in Equation (1) by the value-added coefficient matrix, we will obtain the effect of the port industry expressed in terms of value added, that is,

$$VA_g = D_{VA}\left(I - A^R\right)^{-1}g \qquad (3)$$

As noted previously, the effects on the other important economic variables, such as employment, salaries, gross operating surplus, etc., may be computed in a similar fashion, i.e. by premultiplying the indirect effect on production by the appropriate design matrix containing the relationship between employment, salaries, etc., and gross production for each branch of activity. However, to evaluate the impact of port activity on employment we corrected the coefficients linking employment and production in order to take into account the eventual productivity gains between 2007, the year of the TIO-R, and 2011, the year of our study. The correcting factor uses a measure of apparent productivity of work defined by the GDP per person employed in each of the economic branches of activity. Our estimates are consistent with those employed in studies carried out by the Spanish National Statistics Institute (INE, 2010) and the BBVA Foundation (Fernández de Guevara, 2011).

Regarding the computation of the indirect effect, we need to rely on the information of each geographic destination with a sectoral breakdown of expenditures. In order to do so, in those cases where information directly supplied by companies was not available, the amount spent on purchases and investments was broken down by sectors using the implicit per cent structure in the R-IOT. As a result, we obtained an approximation of the value of intermediate goods and investments that the companies of each sector acquire from the other sectors (or, in some cases, from its own industry) that operate in the same region.

Induced economic effects result from expenditures in private consumption financed by employment remuneration directly and indirectly related to the activity of a port company. In short, the generation of induced effects follows a similar pattern to that of indirect effects, so they can be quantified using a relationship similar to the one contained in Equation (1) used in the case of indirect effects, i.e.

$$y_{induced} = \left(I - A^R\right)^{-1}c\, y_{Induced} = \left(I - A^R\right)^{-1}c \qquad (4)$$

where $y_{induced}$ represents the induced effect on gross production, c is a column vector $n \times 1$ whose characteristic element, c_i, represents the final consumption in goods and services produced by the branch of activity i, by the households of port and dependent industry workers, and by those workers whose jobs were generated by the direct and indirect effects. Consequently, the crucial element in the evaluation of the induced effects is the determination of the consumption impact vector c. For its computation, we first need to specify what proportion of wage remuneration is used for consumption purposes; secondly, we need to know what proportion of the goods and services consumed are supplied by regional companies; and third, we need to determine how the consumption is distributed across the different sectors of the economy.

The consumption factor measures the proportion of the gross remuneration of labour allocated to consumption. The factor is estimated as follows: first, from the official Spanish Accounts (CRE-INE, Región de Murcia. Serie 2008–2010, Cuenta de Renta de los Hogares), which contains the household income accounts, we obtain the figures relative to remuneration of employees, tax collection (income, wealth, company, VAT), and actual and imputed social contributions for the region. The remuneration of employees minus these two items (taxes and social contributions) offers the amount of disposable income, which represents about 56.2% of the total wage bill. Finally, using as a reference the propensity to save of employee disposable income (8.5% according to Arce, Prades, & Urtasun, 2013), we obtain a consumption factor on employee remuneration equal to 51.5%.

Once the direct and indirect impacts of port activity on the remuneration of workers and the consumption factor have been computed, we can directly calculate the total expenditure on consumption made by households. To compute each of the elements entering the impact vector (c), we follow a procedure similar to that seen previously in the case of direct purchases and investments. This implies approximating the geographic and sectoral distribution of expenditures on consumption using the percentage structure of production devoted to final private consumption implicit in the R-IOT.

Furthermore, the induced economic effect on value added is obtained using the previously indicated coefficients which affect this variable. In this way, the induced effect of port activity on value added becomes

$$VA_c = D_{VA}\left(I - A^R\right)^{-1}c \tag{5}$$

The induced effect on the rest of the economic variables of interest (employment, salaries, operating surplus) is calculated in a similar way to that of value added, once we compute the necessary coefficients linking effective production and each of these variables.

Furthermore, we have to modify the computation of the economic effects in order to adjust for inflation. In this regard, note that, whereas all variables in the model were originally defined at current prices of 2011, the R-IOT reflects the relationship between economic variables in 2007. Consequently, in order to gain coherence in the estimation, we opted to evaluate all the variables at 2007 prices in the first step; then the estimated effects were expressed at 2011 prices. In doing so, we used statistical data from INE (CRE Murcia 2008–2012, and CRE Murcia 2000–2012) in order to obtain the necessary deflators with the sectoral breakdown that matches the 35-sector structure of the R-IOT.

Studies on the economic impact of port activities do not usually include a specific analysis of passengers and cruise traffic due to the fact that this type of activity is usually rather small in comparison with the principal operations. Recent studies, however, have begun to focus on the economic effect of cruise tourism due to the importance it is acquiring in Europe.

Within this framework, the economic benefits of cruise industry activity in a given port are derived from the following sources of expenditure:

- The expenditures made by passengers and crew on cruise-related goods and services.
- The expenses of the cruise companies that operate at home ports and ports of call, such as those related to marketing and communication services.
- The expenditures made by cruise lines on goods and services needed for vessel operations, such as food, fuel, navigational and communications equipment, etc.
- The expenditures made in shipyards by cruise lines to allow for the arrival of vessels at the port, as well as on maintenance and repairs.

It is important to underline the differences between expenses associated with cruise activity in home ports and in ports of call. While the former include the outward- and homeward-bound transport expenses, accommodation prior to embarkation, etc., the latter benefit exclusively from the expenditures made during the stopover by passengers and crew, so their impact is smaller. This is the case of cruise tourism in Cartagena since it is currently a port of call, although it is aiming to become a home port in the near future. In general, the economic impact in a port of call comes mainly from the first, second and fourth of the aforementioned sources, with the amount of total expenditure depending on factors such as the duration of the stopover, the amplitude and variety of cultural events and entertainment available in the city of arrival, and the itinerary of the cruise tour operator.

Results

After the arrival of a cruise ship at a port, the cruise company hires the services of a consignee who acts as a representative in each chosen port of call, and is responsible for providing all of the services necessary for the vessel, the passengers and the crew members. The consignee is in charge of administrative, technical and commercial management related to the arrival and departure of the cruise ship, as well as managing embarkation and disembarkation (pilotage, towing and mooring), paperwork with the Maritime Authority and other competent agencies, the rates and fares of the port, medical attention for the crew and monitoring maritime operations, in addition to the supply of provisions and fuel, the hiring of repair companies and other expenditures (health, transport, etc.). The Port Authority receives a series of taxes and tariffs for the services provided to cruises as users of the port facilities. The direct effects for the Port of Cartagena from these activities add up to 1.1 million euros in terms of gross production; 841,000 euros in gross value added; 337,000 euros in gross operating surplus; 520,000 euros in salaries and 8 direct jobs.

While the direct effects are associated with the port services delivered to the cruise ships, the indirect effects include those which proceed from expenditures in the local and regional economy related to the vessel and the cruise industry, as well as any spending on the part of passengers and crew. Accordingly, in order to evaluate the indirect effects, it is crucial to have information on the proportion of port industry activity directly related to cruise visits, plus the amount and distribution of passenger and crew expenditures during the visit. In both cases, the information has been obtained by surveying cruise passengers, crew members, the Port Authority and the dependent industry.

In global terms, the literature points to an average expenditure per passenger in a home port of approximately 290 euros (74 euros if we do not take into account transport to/from the port). In contrast, cruise passengers spend an average of 62 euros in every European port of call (99 euros in those home ports which include guided tours and outings). With regards to crew members, expenditure is concentrated on local shops and restaurants, and amounts to 21 euros for each crew member who disembarks. These figures for the European cruise market are very much in contrast with the estimated average expenditure for other destinations, such as the Canadian Pacific Coast (138 US dollars; Dobson, Gill, & Baird, 2002), or Seattle (180 US dollars; Martin Associates, 2014). In Spain, we have an average expenditure of 49.8 euros for Cádiz (Coronado Guerrero, 2008) and 62.6 euros for Malaga (de Málaga, 2013).

According to the survey conducted by the Port Authority of Cartagena, each cruise passenger spends an average of 2 h and 21 min visiting the city and spends approximately 25 euros. Moreover, in this study we rely on the following assumptions regarding expenditures by passengers and crew members who visit the city:

- 5% of cruise passengers do not disembark during stopovers, and of those that do, 10% do not spend any money at all.
- 50% of the crew disembark during stopovers, and of these, 10% do not spend any money. The average expenditure of each crew member is equal to 40% of that of the average passenger.
- A total of 88,081 passengers came to the Port of Cartagena in 2011; the number of crew members was roughly half that number.

The estimated sectorial distribution of the expenditures of the cruise passengers that visited the Port of Cartagena in 2011 is shown in Table 2. It includes an expenditure structure similar to the one characterising those cruise ports of call of similar size in Europe and Spain (see Coronado Guerrero, 2008), with a few particular differences in the case of Cartagena.

The indirect impact figures show estimates of 3.3 million euros for gross production, 1.9 million for gross value added, 45 indirect jobs, 903,000 euros in indirect salaries and 1 million euros for gross operating surplus. By sectors, the indirect effects are concentrated on those that receive passenger and crew member expenditures, such as shops, hotels and restaurants, leisure and cultural services, rental services and the agro-food industry. Local shops and tourism-related services are the sectors that generate most employment.

The induced effects result from the direct and indirect remunerations for the port industry from cruise-related activities, together with the induced impact from the remunerations received by workers in companies where cruise passengers and crew make purchases. The estimations we obtained imply that the induced effects reach 651,000 euros in production, 357,000 euros in gross value added, 7 jobs, 162,000 euros in salaries and 192,000 euros in gross operating surplus. The sectoral profile is mainly concentrated on shopping, real-estate activities, and hotels and restaurants.

The total effects, displayed in Table 3, are calculated as the sum of the direct, indirect and induced effects, accounting for approximately 5 million euros in 2011 in terms of production, 3.1 million in gross value added, 60 jobs, 1.6 million euros in salaries and 1.5 million euros in gross operating surplus. The sectors most directly involved in cruise tourism-related operations are those of shopping, transport services, real estate activities, and hotels and restaurants. In relation to the regional economy, cruise activities generate 0.012% of the gross value added, 0.11% of regional employment, 0.012% of salaries and 0.013% of gross operating surplus (Table 4).

Conclusions and implications

The cruise industry has grown significantly during the last decade in the European and Spanish markets. More than 30 million passengers arrived at European ports in 2013, with 7.6 million visiting Spanish ports. As a result, a growing number of studies set out to quantify the economic impact of the cruise industry in a given area.

In this paper we build on a regional IO framework in order to improve the methodology usually employed in this type of analysis. In doing so, we have followed a two-stage procedure: firstly, we have collected survey data in order to compute the direct expenditure of passengers and operators (crew and vessel expenses); and, secondly, we have employed the R-IOT to strictly compute the indirect and induced economic effects of cruise activity. To the best of our knowledge, this is the first study to build on an accurate regional framework in order to calculate the economic impact of the cruise industry on the regional economy linked to the port.

Table 2. Sectorial distribution of expenditure by passengers and crew (% of total expenditure).

Sector	Passengers (%)	Crew (%)
Wholesale and retail trade	37	25
Accommodation and food services activities	34	65
Transportation	8	0
Travel agency and tour operator activities	3	0
Cultural and recreational services	15	0
Telecommunications	1.5	5
Financial and insurance activities	1.5	5
Total	100	100

Source: Own elaboration based on survey data, and Coronado Guerrero (2008).

Table 3. Total effects of cruise tourism on the regional economy 2011.

		Gross production	Gross added value	Employment	Wages and salaries	Gross operating surplus
AA,BB	Agriculture, forestry and fishing	4587.2	2901.6	0.1	885.7	2093.2
CA,CB	Mining and quarrying	1717.9	678.7	0.0	343.4	338.0
DA	Manufacture of food products, beverages and tobacco products	48419.0	11060.3	0.2	7743.3	3345.7
DB	Manufacture of textiles and wearing apparel	4253.9	1042.4	0.0	642.8	409.0
DC	Manufacture of leather and related products	830.5	153.4	0.0	95.0	60.0
DD	Manufacture of wood and of products of wood and cork	8768.2	1821.1	0.0	1136.9	721.6
DE	Manufacture of paper and paper products; printing and reproduction of recorded media	14372.9	4787.4	0.1	3206.6	1612.7
DG	Manufacture of chemicals and chemical products	660.6	160.3	0.0	77.1	83.1
DH	Manufacture of rubber and plastic products	2834.7	688.6	0.0	599.6	91.6
DI	Manufacture of other non-metallic mineral products	13382.8	3437.0	0.1	1730.6	1696.8
DJ	Manufacture of basic metals and fabricated metal products	28729.5	8873.1	0.2	5243.3	3707.9
DK	Manufacture of machinery and equipment	2176.3	725.7	0.0	401.4	330.7
DL	Manufacture of electrical equipment, computer, electronic and optical products	3026.2	550.7	0.0	411.4	144.1
DM	Manufacture of transport equipment	57977.3	11783.6	0.2	5379.3	6614.8
DN	Other manufactures	11557.5	2764.8	0.1	2234.7	564.0
DF, EE	Electricity, gas, steam and water supply	144499.3	31194.8	0.1	6326.1	24183.9
FF	Construction	213453.5	86234.3	1.5	45900.6	39597.3
GG	Wholesale and retail trade and repair of motor vehicles	1555770.0	934605.3	28.5	500173.0	437913.7
HH	Accommodation and food service activities	375587.5	240253.7	4.6	99935.2	140366.1
II	Passenger rail transport	559.7	263.1	0.0	120.9	141.8
II	Freight rail transport	1.4	0.6	0.0	0.3	0.3
II	Passenger air transport	0.0	0.0	0.0	0.0	0.0
II	Freight air transport	0.0	0.0	0.0	0.0	0.0
II	Passenger road transport	406513.4	298266.7	5.6	137018.6	160729.0
II	Freight transport by rail	63487.8	34142.4	0.6	15684.4	18398.5
II	Passenger water transport	0.0	0.0	0.0	0.0	0.0
II	Freight water transport	4.2	2.7	0.0	1.2	1.5
II	Warehousing and support activities for transportation	1093838.1	855936.8	8.3	509384.5	345062.6
II	Telecommunications	38573.2	14106.2	0.5	6480.1	7601.5
JJ	Financial and insurance activities	91253.9	60685.5	0.5	24850.6	35437.1
KK	Real estate activities; professional, scientific and technical activities; support and administrative service activities	573319.7	353981.6	3.6	88733.5	254990.4
LL	Public administration and defence; compulsory social security	15.8	10.6	0.0	8.2	2.3
MM	Education	16852.2	14908.4	0.3	12545.4	2361.3
NN	Human health activities	62118.1	43361.4	0.9	34760.9	8578.4
OO, PP, QQ	Other personal service activities	153503.3	98577.3	3.4	54715.7	43585.4
	Total	4992645.7	3117959.7	59.7	1566770.4	1540764.3

Source: Own elaboration.

Table 4. Total effects by type: contribution to the economy of the Region of Murcia 2011.

	Gross production	Gross added value	Employment	Wages and salaries	Gross operating surplus
Direct effects	1056998.4	840913.6	8.0	502483.1	336967.0
Indirect effects	3284885.5	1919972.2	44.6	902570.1	1011306.9
Induced effects	650761.7	357073.9	7.1	161717.2	192490.4
Total effects	4992645.7	3117959.7	59.7	1566770.4	1540764.3
% Region of Murcia		0.0122%	0.0109%	0.0118%	0.0127%

Source: Own elaboration.

Finally, in order to illustrate the performance of this methodological framework, we have applied it to the Port of Cartagena, Spain. The detailed information provided by the IO framework has allowed us to rigorously estimate the direct, indirect and induced effects arising from the cruise industry. It has also helped us to identify the economic impact of the cruise industry on the sectors involved in these activities. To sum up, we have been able to extend and refine the method of computing the economic impact of cruise activities on a regional rather than solely a national level. Our main aim has been to provide a methodological benchmark for the benefit of future studies.

Acknowledgement

Prof. Andrés Artal-Tur acknowledges the financial support by Groups of Excellence of the Region of Murcia, Fundación Séneca, Science and Technology Agency, Project 19,884/GERM/15.

Disclosure statement

No potential conflict of interest was reported by the authors.

Funding

Prof. Andrés Artal-Tur acknowledges the financial support by Groups of Excellence of the Region of Murcia, Fundación Séneca, Science and Technology Agency, [Project 19884/GERM/15]. The authors also thank financial aid from FEMISE Association [Project ENPI/2014/354-494] with Research Projects [FEM 41-04 and FEM 41-13].

ORCID

Andrés Artal-Tur (iD) http://orcid.org/0000-0003-3423-8570
José Miguel Navarro-Azorín (iD) http://orcid.org/0000-0001-9698-1226
José María Ramos-Parreño (iD) http://orcid.org/0000-0003-2007-0834

References

Arce, O., Prades, E., & Urtasun, A. (2013, September). *La evolución del ahorro y del consumo de los hogares españoles durante la crisis* [Trends in saving and consumption of Spanish households along the economic crisis]. Madrid: Boletín Económico, Banco de España.
BREA. (2013). *The economic contribution of Cruise Tourism in Victoria 2012.* Exton: PA: Business Research & Economic Advisors.
Brida, J. G., Bukstein, D., Garrido, E., Tealde, E., & Zapata, S. (2010). Impactos económicos del turismo de cruceros. Un análisis del gasto de los pasajeros de cruceros que visitan el Caribe colombiano [Economic impact of cruise tourism in the Columbian Caribbean]. *Estudios y Perspectivas en Turismo, 19*, 5.
Brida, J. G., Bukstein, D., & Tealde, E. (2012). Patrones de gasto de cruceristas en dos puertos uruguayos [Cruise expenditure pattern in two Uruguayan ports]. *Estudios y Perspectivas en Turismo, 21*, 5.

Brida, J. G., & Zapata, S. (2010a). Economic impacts of cruise tourism: The case of Costa Rica. *Anatolia: An International Journal of Tourism and Hospitality Research, 21*(2), 322–338.

Brida, J. G., & Zapata, S. (2010b). Cruise tourism: Economic, socio-cultural and environmental impacts. *International Journal of Leisure and Tourism Marketing, 1*(3), 205–226.

Chase, G. L., & McKee, D. L. (2003). The economic impact of cruise tourism on Jamaica. *Journal, of Tourism Studies, 14*(2), 16–22.

CLIA. (2015). *Contribution of Cruise Tourism to the Economies of Europe 2015 Edition*. Brussels: Cruise Lines International Association Europe.

Coronado Guerrero, D. (ed.). (2008). *Evaluación del impacto económico del Puerto de la Bahía de Cádiz* [Evaluating the economic impact of Bahia de Cadiz Port]. Cádiz: Universidad de Cádiz.

Cruise Lines International Association (CLIA) (2017). State of the industry. Cruise Lines International Association Europe. Retrieved from https://www.cruising.org/about-the-industry/research/2017-state-of-the-industry

de Málaga, P. (2013). *Análisis del Turismo de Cruceros 2012* [Cruise tourism outlook in 2012]. Málaga: Autoridad Portuaria de Málaga y Sociedad de Planificación y Desarrollo (SOPDE).

Dobson, S., Gill, A., & Baird, S. (2002). *A primer on the canadian pacific Cruise ship industry*. Vancouver: Simon Fraser University.

Dwyer, L., & Forsyth, P. (1998). Economic significance of cruise tourism. *Annals of Tourism Research, 25*(2), 393–415.

Fernández de Guevara, J. (2011). *La productividad sectorial en España. Una perspectiva micro* [The productiviy of economic sectors in Spain: A micro perspective]. Bilbao: Fundación BBVA.

Gibson, P., & Bentley, M. (2006). A study of impacts-cruise tourism and the South West of England. *Journal of Travel & Tourism Marketing, 20*(3/4), 63–77.

INE. (2010). *La productividad industrial en España. Panorámica de la Industria* [The productivity in the industrial sector in Spain]. Madrid: Instituto Nacional de Estadística.

Llano, C. (1998). Un modelo Input-Output interregional para Europa: Una visión intersectorial de las relaciones de dependencia comercial intra-UE [An interregional input-output model for Europe]. (Doctoral Dissertation). Universidad Autónoma de Madrid, Madrid.

Llano, C. (2004). Economía espacial y sectorial: El comercio interregional en el contexto de un modelo multi-regional para la economía española [The inter-regional trade flows in the context of a multiregional model for the Spanish economy]. Instituto de Estudios Fiscales, Ministerio de Economía y Hacienda. In *Colección de Investigaciones nº 1/04*.

Martin Associates. (2014). The 2013 economic impact of the port of Seattle, Retrieved from http://www.portseattle.org/Supporting-Our-Community/Economic-Development/Documents/2014_economic_impact_report_martin.pdf

Quan-Novelo, A., Santoya, J., & Vellos, R. (2007). *Assessing the direct economic impact of Cruise Tourism on the Belizean economy*. Belize City: Research Department, Central Bank of Belize.

State Port Authority (2005–2016). Ministry of Fomento (Spain), Retrieved from www.puertos.es

Vina, L. D. L., & Ford, J. (1998). Economic impact of proposed cruise ship business. *Annals of Tourism Research, 25*(4), 205–208.

Worley, T., & Akehurst, G. (2013). *Economic impact of the New Zealand cruise sector*. Auckland: Market Economics Limited.

Profiling cruise passengers in a Mediterranean port-of-call

Annarita Sorrentino ⓘ, Marcello Risitano ⓘ, Giacomo Del Chiappa ⓘ and Tindara Abbate ⓘ

ABSTRACT

This study profiles cruise passengers based on their perceived satisfaction with their experience. Exploratory factor analysis (EFA) and K-means Cluster Analysis were applied to a sample of 419 cruise passengers interviewed in the period March–April 2013 at the port-of-call of Messina (Italy). The main factors that influenced destination satisfaction were: onshore shopping experience, transportation and tourist services, security perceptions, port-related factors, length of stay, and aesthetic perceptions of the destination. Furthermore, two clusters were identified: "independent passengers" and "organized passengers". Contributions to the body of knowledge and managerial implications are discussed and suggestions for further research are given.

Introduction

In the last two decades, the cruise industry has undergone significant expansion (Ozturk & Gogtas, 2016). Within the next four years, 50 cruise ships will enter the market, adding 148,000 beds to the existing global offering (Italian Cruise Watch, 2016). The cruise trip is nowadays a choice of vacation for every market segment, including singles and young people, because of low pricing strategies and new itineraries; moreover, some customized services and entertainment have transformed what was commonly perceived to be a luxury but potentially boring product into a more widely desired tourism experience (De Cantis, Ferrante, Kahani, & Shoval, 2016).

This form of tourism is interesting to observe from different perspectives. For instance, the analysis of cruise passengers' behaviours and their impacts on a sea-port destination is relevant to policy makers and destination marketers. Furthermore, the analysis of cruise passengers' behaviour on excursions when the ship is in harbour is important because of the influence of their experiences on passengers satisfaction, their intention to return as a tourist (not necessarily on a cruise), and their intention to recommend the destination to others (both offline and online) (Andriotis & Agiomirgianakis, 2010, 2013; Brida, Pulina, Riaño, & Zapata-Aguirre, 2012b; De Cantis et al., 2016; Parola, Satta, Penco, & Persico, 2014).

Several studies have analysed cruise passengers behaviour and satisfaction with their inland experiences, but few have done so in the Italian context (e.g. Satta, Parola, Penco, & Persico, 2015). This study was therefore carried out to deepen the current literature on cruise tourism by proposing a segmentation approach to the study of cruiser passengers' behaviours in the city of Messina, a Mediterranean port-of-call in Italy. In 2015, Messina was ranked as the tenth Italian port in terms of passenger numbers, with 327,706 passengers (3%) and 160 (3.3%) ship calls and the second port of the Sicily region, after Palermo.

The paper aims to discover the dimensions of the inland experience for cruise passengers that shape their satisfaction and behavioural intentions and to investigate whether differences among clusters of factors exist based on their socio-demographic characteristics as well as trip characteristics (length of stay and trip motivation).

Literature review

Cruise passenger behaviour at a destination has been studied only recently (Andriotis & Agiomirgianakis, 2010; Brida, Bukstein, Garrido, & Tealde, 2012a; Brida et al., 2013, 2012b; De Cantis et al., 2016). As the itinerary is one of the main reasons why people choose a particular cruise (Henthorne, 2000), the analysis of the sea-port experience assumes a particular relevance. Such analysis should encompass not only the short-term economic impacts (Braun, Xander, & White, 2002; Chase & Alon, 2002; McKee & Chase, 2003) but also the passengers' behaviours, their perceived satisfaction, and their intention to return to the destination as inland tourist and to recommend it to others: the so-called show casing effect (Gabe, Lynch, & McConnon, 2006). This perspective can be considered crucial for policy makers in order to improve the tourist facilities and design new services.

Previous studies of cruise passenger behaviour at destination have made a distinction between *home-port* and *port-of-call* cruise tourism destinations. The home-port is where a cruise trip starts and ends (Brida et al., 2012b). Ports of call are destinations at which passengers can disembark to spend some time (typically between 4 and 8 h) visiting the main attractions, shopping or enjoying a local tour organized by the cruise line company. Previous studies (e.g. Brida & Zapata, 2010) have shown that the overall economic impact is higher for home-port cruise tourism destinations. Researchers investigating the onshore experience have given attention to the economic expenditures of passengers and their expectations, satisfaction and behavioural intentions. They have found a positive relationship between destination satisfaction and the likelihood of a passenger returning to the destination and recommending it to others (Parola et al., 2014). Parola et al. (2014) also identified the role of the excursion package as a moderator in the formation of satisfaction, and demonstrated that people who go on an organized onshore tour are more likely to return to that destination in the future.

A recent work on the port-of-call of Messina showed that satisfaction, nationality and length of stay can be considered as proxies of the total expenditure (Gargano & Grasso, 2016) demonstrating a significant difference of expenditure in relation to the perceived satisfaction. In particular, the authors showed that the expenditure is influenced by different factors in the sub-groups of cruise ship visitors such as satisfaction, nationality, length of stay and season.

Using multivariate analysis (correspondence analysis, hierarchical cluster analysis), most studies on cruise tourist behaviour at port-of-call destinations has focused on the segmentation of passengers in order to identify possible sub-groups with homogeneous behaviours (2013; Brida et al., 2012b, 2012c; De Cantis et al., 2016). Factors affecting the onshore experience have been reported to be satisfaction, perceived safety and security, and the onshore activities (Andriotis & Agiomirgianakis, 2010; Brida, Scuderi, & Seijas, 2014), as well as the length of stay at the destination (Henthorne, 2000).

This paper contributes to tourist behaviour analysis in cruise marketing studies and provides new empirical evidence. The main objectives are to describe cruise passenger behaviour during the onshore experience (e.g. traveller profile, trip motivation, land expenditure, overall satisfaction), to identify patterns in perceived satisfaction through an exploratory factor analysis (EFA), and to classify cruise tourists into homogeneous groups derived from the factor scores in the EFA.

Methodology

Messina has been chosen as the context of this study because it has recently emerged as an important port on Mediterranean cruise itineraries, from South to North and from East to West. Cruise companies that take in Messina as a port-of-call include: Carnival Cruises, Royal Caribbean, Princess Cruise, Cunard, P&O and Celebrity Cruises. Messina is a home port for MSC Cruises. The appeal of this destination derives from its historical interest (e.g. monuments and buildings), the landscape, its ethnic appeal and local folklore, and high-quality local wine and food (with visits to producers). A wide variety of cruise routes are possible to and from Messina, and the mild climate extends the tourist season year round.

MSC Cruises is an Italian cruise line company and the fourth largest cruise line and the largest privately owned company in the world, after Carnival Cruises, Royal Caribbean and Norwegian Cruise Lines; it had a 5.2% share of all passengers carried in 2015 and was the market leader in the Mediterranean, South America and South Africa. The company, which grew by 800% from 2004 to 2014, carried 1.67 million guests in 2014 and reported strong financial results, with a turnover of €1.5 billion.

Cruise tourism is an important sector of the tourism industry in Messina. As described in Table 1, the number of passenger arrivals in Messina increased from 216,270 in 2005 to 501,316 in 2013. In 2016, 187 ships bringing 377,112 passengers were booked to call, including 13 ships that had never been to the Sicilian port city before (MedCruise, 2016). According to the Observatory on Tourism on European Islands (OTIE, 2009), average spending is around €50–70 with an average expenditure on excursions of €20–30.

Data collection and analysis

For the purposes of this study, a passenger survey instrument was developed based on prior studies (e.g. Brida et al., 2012a, 2013) complemented with input from discussions with principal actors in the cruise industry in the city, such as port managers and local and national government tourism officials. The questionnaire has four main sections. The first is focused on socio-

Table 1. Cruise passenger arrivals in Messina, 1995–2015.

Year	Cruise Passengers	% change (year on year)
1995	26,959	
1996	35,484	31.62%
1997	76,137	114.57%
1998	120,600	58.40%
1999	111,868	−7.24%
2000	126,023	12.65%
2001	112,675	−10.59%
2002	145,647	29.26%
2003	229,276	57.42%
2004	204,380	−10.86%
2005	216,270	5.82%
2006	253,462	17.20%
2007	293,296	15.72%
2008	337,117	14.94%
2009	253,199	−24.89%
2010	374,441	47.88%
2011	500,636	33.70%
2012	438,379	−12.44%
2013	501,316	14.36%
2014	319,750	−36.22%
2015	327,702	2.49%

Source: Port Authority (2016).

demographic information (e.g. nationality, country of residence, marital status, education level, gross annual household income). The second section asks respondents to give information about their trip, such as the main reasons for choosing it, how they bought the cruise trip and their cruise experiences before this. The third section comprises questions about the passengers' expenditure behaviours. Finally, the fourth section asks passengers to express their satisfaction with the port of Messina. Passengers recorded their responses on a 5-point *Likert* scale ranging from "very dissatisfied" to "very satisfied". They were asked to indicate their perception of their personal safety and security on a four-point *Likert* scale, ranging from "very unsafe" to "very safe". Following a review of official statistics on the nationalities of cruise passengers arriving at the port of Messina, the questionnaire was translated into English. The questionnaire was pilot tested on a sample of 25 passengers to verify the validity of its content, the comprehensibility of the questions, and scale. No concerns were reported in the pilot tests. Data were collected face to face in the period March–April 2013 by two trained interviewers directly supervised by the authors. At the end of the data collection, 462 responses from cruise passengers aged over 18 years were obtained. After eliminating those with missing data, 419 responses were usable for the statistical analysis.

Data were analysed using different techniques with SPSS 23. Firstly, descriptive analysis was carried out to define: the socio-demographic and traveller profile of the respondents; and passenger behaviour at the destination (e.g. satisfaction with the onshore experience and onshore expenditure). Secondly, an EFA was implemented to find factors that influence passenger satisfaction. Thirdly, a *k-means* cluster analysis was conducted to verify if and how level of satisfaction could define homogeneous market segments, and a bivariate analysis was then done to get a better understanding of the clusters obtained.

Results

The majority of the respondents were not Italian nationals (72.73%) and 30.9% were Italian. More than 43% were in the 26–45 age range but a large group of respondents were over 56 years old (35.6%). Most respondents were married (68.7%). Approximately 43% had a college or university degree, and 14% had undertaken postgraduate studies. In terms of income, the two largest groups were those with an annual income in the range €26,000–€50,000 (28.9% or respondents) and those on less than <€25,000 (22%).

The traveller profile

The majority of the passengers were travelling with a partner (54.9%) or relatives (20%). The sample consists of 50.8% of passengers who were travelling for the first-time cruisers and the 48.7% of repeat cruisers with an average of three previous cruise trips. The majority of respondents (53.7%) had used a travel agency to purchase the cruise package. The mean onboard expenditure per capita was about €53 per day. Finally, a large part of the sample (40.9%) were travelling with the Italian group MSC, while the rest of the sample were travelling on foreign cruise ships. Respondents were also asked to specify the main purpose of the cruise trip by indicating a score on a 7-point Likert scale (1 = extremely important; 7 = not important at all). The motivation "to visit different cities" had the lowest score (i.e. was rated most important) (2.7), followed by the statements "because of a planned itinerary" and "because of a favourable price" (both 3.7). The motivation receiving the lowest score was "cruise services and facilities".

Passenger behaviour at destination

The majority of respondents visited Messina for the first time (61.9%), but a large part of the sample already knew the destination (38.1%), with an average of 1.7 previous visits. This finding is understandable given the significant presence of Italian passengers in the sample. Most of the sample spent between 2 (34.7%) and 4 (29.4%) hours at the destination. During the onshore experience, passengers had two options: to join a cruise line sponsored bus tour, usually involving visits to the historical centre and the main archaeological and cultural attractions; or to explore the destination on their own (Andriotis & Agiomirgianakis, 2010). Passengers visited on average more than three tourist places and almost all respondents visited the historical centre (94.5%). The most visited tourist attractions were the main churches and the regional museum (26%). These findings influenced the overall onshore satisfaction.

Onshore satisfaction

The destination visiting experience is considered as one of a key determinant of tourist satisfaction, especially in the case of cruise passengers because they have typically just a few hours to enjoy a destination In this study, tourists were asked to express the level of satisfaction in relation to the 22 items reported in Table 2 as explained in the methodology section.

As Table 4 shows, there are a lot of missing values which represent the score "no opinion"; this reduces the mean scores, especially those related to the overall shopping experience. However, the overall satisfaction was reasonably good (3.5). The highest scores were for the items the "weather" and "friendliness of local people", which agrees with the literature on Mediterranean cruise ports (Andriotis & Agiomirgianakis, 2010; Brida et al., 2012b). The lowest satisfaction was expressed about "street vendors", "cleanliness of the city" and "traffic and noise".

Respondents were also asked to express their level of perceived personal security on five items: port; personal; tours; taxi; street. The respondents expressed an overall good level of perceived

Table 2. Overall perceived satisfaction.

		Extremely dissatisfied				Extremely dissatisfied		
		1	2	3	4	5	Mean	SD
1.	The weather	4.1	2.9	23	45	25.1	3.84	0.97
2.	Friendliness of people	2.6	2.9	29.4	43.8	21.3	3.78	0.90
3.	Time to visit Messina	3.3	6.5	23.7	49.8	16.7	3.70	0.94
4.	Initial shore-side welcome	4.8	3.8	25.8	49.8	15.8	3.68	0.95
5.	Harbour facilities and services	3.8	4.3	29.9	48.8	13.2	3.63	0.90
6.	Tourist information	2.2	5.5	36.8	39.2	16.3	3.62	0.90
7.	Historic centre decorum	3.6	8.1	29.7	45.5	13.2	3.56	0.94
8.	Courtesy of sales people	2.9	2.2	44.7	38.8	11.5	3.54	0.83
9.	Variety of typical local products	2.6	2.4	49.5	35.6	9.8	3.48	0.81
10.	Variety of goods	2.9	3.1	47.6	36.4	10	3.48	0.83
11.	Quality of products offered	2.9	4.1	44.5	39	9.6	3.48	0.83
12.	Variety of tourist attractions	3.3	5.7	43.3	36.8	10.8	3.46	0.88
13.	Price	2.6	5.7	45	38	8.6	3.44	0.83
14.	Shopping infrastructure	3.1	3.8	50.5	34.4	8.1	3.41	0.82
15.	Shopping experience	3.3	4.3	49.8	34	8.6	3.40	0.84
16.	Communication ability of drivers, guides, etc.	2.4	3.3	57.2	26.6	10.5	3.39	0.81
17.	Tour guide	1.9	2.4	61.2	25.6	8.9	3.37	0.76
18.	Transport (buses and taxis)	3.6	2.6	57.4	26.8	9.6	3.36	0.83
19.	Bus and taxi drivers	2.4	1.7	66	21.3	8.6	3.32	0.75
20.	Cleanliness of the city	14.8	14.8	26.1	34.2	10.8	3.13	1.21
21.	Street vendors	10	13.2	46.4	21.8	8.6	3.06	1.05
22.	Traffic and noise	17.5	20.8	28.7	24.6	8.4	2.86	1.21
Safety and security level in the following places								
23.	Port	4.0	2.8	20.4	58.4	14.4	3.8	0.9
24.	Personal	3.7	4.2	27.8	48.6	15.7	3.7	0.9
25.	Tours	3.3	1.8	43.1	36.7	15.1	3.6	0.9
26.	Taxi	3.6	2.4	45.9	34.5	13.5	3.5	0.9
27.	Street	5.1	8.1	32.0	42.4	12.4	3.5	1.0

SD, standard deviation

security (3.6). The highest score was for security in the port and the lowest score was for security in the street.

Even short destination visits can generate a positive or negative memorable experience (Gabe et al., 2006) and affect the probability of returning to the destination or recommending it to others. The analysis of the intentional behaviours is important to help cruise companies and destination managers improve cruise facilities and services for cruise visitors. Respondents were therefore asked to indicate their willingness to recommend Messina to others and to return to the city themselves. More than half the sample (55%) were willing to recommend the destination and 35% would return. It is likely that the low probability of return was mediated by the low satisfaction on some critical factors, as satisfaction and intention to return are normally positively correlated (Bigne, Sanchez, & Sanchez, 2001; Prayag, 2009; Yoon & Uysal, 2005).

Onshore expenditure

The onshore expenditure is presented in Table 3. The average total expenditure was €39 per passenger, with most of the money spent on food and drink (the mean, though, was not the highest for this item because 84% of people spent less than €40 on it). The highest average was related to the guided tour; of those who took the tour, 83% spent <€100 and 17% between €101 and €400. It is interesting that the expenditure on jewellery (24.4% of all onshore expenditure) was higher than that on souvenirs (19.0%). The expenditure on internet and mobile phone was surprisingly high, at €52 on average, but this might be linked to the "roaming" charge paid by foreigners.

Exploratory factor analysis

EFA was performed on the 27 satisfaction and security items to reveal any underlying patterns. The Kaiser–Mayer–Olkin measure of sampling adequacy was 0.896 and Barlett's test of sphericity was significant ($p = .00$). The communalities were all above 0.6, confirming that each item shared some common variance with other items. Principal component analysis was used as the extraction method because the main purpose was to verify factors underlying passenger satisfaction and perceived security. Varimax rotation was used because factor scores were used in the analysis. A five-factor preferred solution was confirmed by Kaiser's rule (eigenvalues >1), scree-plot and parallel analysis (Cattell & Vogelmann, 1977; Horn, 1965). The eigenvalues ranged from 1.016 and 8.680, meaning that the five constructs explain 79.9% of the total variance. Cronbach's alpha for the five factors varied from 0.81 to 0.90, suggesting great internal consistency. Factor loadings of the variables ranged from 0.715 to 0.900, above the suggested threshold value of 0.30 for practical and statistical significance (Hair, Anderson,

Table 3. The onshore expenditure.

Onshore expenditure	Min	Max	Mean	Sum per category	% of all expenditure
Tour guided	5	400	€55.78	€4072.00	15.8
Internet/mobile phone	4	120	€52.00	€884.00	7.3
Museum	5	160	€44.25	€354.00	3.5
Typical products	10	150	€38.00	€190.00	2.2
Jewellery	1	500	€29.77	€3364.50	24.4
Food & drink	4	232	€31.98	€5509.25	49.3
Souvenirs	3	80	€22.81	€1003.80	19.0
Pharmacy/health	1	50	€11.12	€734.20	28.5
Local transportation	2	40	€10.18	€173.00	7.3

Table 4. Exploratory factor analysis.

Construct and items	Factor loadings	Mean	Eigenvalue	% Variance explained	% Cumulative variance	Cronbach's α	Communalities
Onshore shopping experience			8.680	26.1	26.1	0.86	
1. Variety of typical local products	.883	3.48					.854
2. Variety of goods	.882	3.48					.864
3. Quality of goods	.875	3.48					.836
4. Shopping infrastructure	.846	3.41					.792
5. Courtesy of sales people	.789	3.54					.752
6. Price	.715	3.44					.622
7. Shopping experience	.698	3.40					.602
Transportation & tourist services			2.567	17.5	43.7	0.90	
8. Bus and taxi drivers	.900	3.32					.909
9. Communication ability of drivers, guides, etc.	.874	3.39					.865
10. Tour guide	.868	3.37					.855
11. Transport (buses and taxis)	.807	3.36					.829
Security perception			1.988	15.4	59	0.82	
12. Tours	.884	3.58					.875
13. Personal	.861	3.69					.789
14. Taxi	.846	3.52					.815
15. Harbour	.741	3.76					.651
Port-related factors and time in destination			1.722	12	71	0.81	
16. Harbour facilities and services	.849	3.63					.863
17. Initial shore-side welcome	.846	3.68					.840
18. Time to visit Messina	.725	3.70					.684
Aesthetic perception of the destination			1.016	8.9	79.9	0.84	
19. Traffic and noise	.887	2.86					.853
20. Cleanliness of the city	.855	3.13					.823
Total % of variance explained			79.9%				

Tatham, & Black, 1984). Table 4 shows the percentage variance explained by each factor. A total of seven items were eliminated because cross-loadings.

The final solution (Table 4) comprises five latent variables that determine the manifest indicators and fits the constructs of satisfaction and security perception. Factors were labelled by reflecting the meaning of the items. Factor 1 is the most important, as it explains the 26.1% of the total variance. It was named "Onshore shopping experience" and has seven items: variety of typical local products (mean factor loading = 3.48), variety of goods (3.48), quality of goods (3.48), shopping infrastructure (3.41), courtesy of sales people (3.54), price (3.44) and shopping experience (3.40). This factor reflects the overall satisfaction derived from the shopping experience at the destination, which is an important part of the onshore visit. Factor 2 was named "Transportation and tourist services" and it has four items: bus and taxi drivers (3.32), communication ability of guides and drivers (3.39), tour guide (3.37) and transport (buses and taxis) (3.36). This factor reveals the satisfaction derived from the interaction with human resources in tourism services and the quality of local transportation. Factor 3 summarizes the latent construct of level of perceived security and it initially consisted of five items, but the item related to security in the street crossed two factors and it was deleted because of overload, leaving the four listed in Table 6. Factor 4 was named "Port-related factors and length of stay" and it consists of three items: harbour facilities and services (3.63), initial shore-side welcome (3.68) and time to visit Messina (3.70).

This factor is related to the perceived satisfaction with the basic cruise facilities and welcoming services for cruise passengers who disembark at the port-of-call, including the time allowed by the company to enjoy the onshore visit. The last factor was named

"Esthetic perception of the destination" and it has two items: traffic and noise (2.86 and cleanliness of the city (3.13).

Cluster analysis

The cluster analysis, carried out using a non-hierarchical classification (*k-means* method), with the factors obtained, identifies two groups of passengers. To infer the correct cluster number, a pseudo-F test was conducted (Caliński & Harabasz, 1974). It suggested the two-cluster solution as the optimal one, with an F-value of 88.229 (all p-values<.00). Table 5 shows the final centroids and proportion of the two clusters. Note that positive and negative scores on the specific dimensions indicate higher or lower than average traits within the clusters. We labelled passengers belonging to cluster 1 "Independent cruisers". This group contains 154 passengers (36.8%) and shows the lowest scores on the aesthetic perception of the destination and port-related factors and length of stay, while they demonstrate the highest scores on security perception, transport and tourist services and the onshore shopping experience.

Cluster 2 was labelled "Organized cruisers". This group represents 63.2% of the sample, with 264 passengers. It seems exactly opposite to the first cluster and it shows the highest average scores on the port-related factors, the length of stay and the aesthetic perception of the destination, while they appear to be unsatisfied with the onshore shopping experience, and the local transport and the tourist services; they perceived a lower level of security.

Comparative analysis

In a second step, we computed cross-tabulations to describe clusters of passengers in terms of their socio-demographic characteristics and onshore expenditure. There were no significant differences between groups in the following variables: age, means of cruise purchase, onboard expenditure and the segmentation between first-time cruisers and repeat cruisers. Table 6 shows only the significant results of the cross-tabulations and t-test related to the cluster.

Table 5. K-means cluster analysis.

	Cluster	
	Independent cruisers	Organized cruisers
N	154	265
%	36.8%	63.2%
Onshore shopping experience	.322	−.187
Transportation & tourist services	.804	−.469
Security perception	.138	−.080
Port-related factors and time at destination	−.284	.166
Aesthetic perception of the destination	−.671	.391

Table 6. Comparative analysis.

	Independent cruisers	*N*	%	Organized cruisers	*N*	%	*p*-Value
Nationality	Italian	85	55.1%	Foreigners	201	77%	.00
Education	High school	84	54.4%	Degree	133	50.3%	.00
Income	<25k	44	28.5%	26–50k	87	32.9%	.00
Cruise company	MSC	89	57.8%	Others	179	68.1%	.00
Time spent at destination	2–3	75	48.7%	3–4	89	34%	.00
	Mean independent cruisers		**Mean organized cruisers**				
Willingness to repeat a cruise	2.94		3.28				.00
Willingness to return to Messina	2.75		3.13				.00
Willingness to recommend Messina	3.48		3.46				1.91

Cluster 1, labelled "Independent cruisers", tends to consist of Italian people (55.1%), the majority with a medium-high education level and an annual income <€25k; they are mostly MSC passengers and they have spent 2–3 h in Messina. Cluster 2, labelled "Organized passengers", is mainly foreigners (77%), with a high education level and a higher annual income than the first cluster; they spent more than 3 h in Messina and they were not MSC cruisers.

In addition, two one-way ANOVAs were carried out to verify a potential variance from clusters related to the cruise trip motivation and the onshore expenditure categories. Both analyses revealed a significant variance (p-value .00). The motivation was significant on the items "to visit different cities" and the item "because of the competitive price", in particular cluster 1, "independent cruisers", shows a higher mean (3.2) for the motivation price competitiveness, while cluster 2, "organized cruisers", shows a higher mean (2.4) for the motivation "to visit different cities". The one-way ANOVA related to the *onshore* expenditure revealed a significant variance between the two clusters on the item related to expenditure on the guided tour (p-value .00). In particular, the independent cruisers showed a low average expenditure (€28), while the organized cruisers showed a higher average (65 €). The overall onshore expenditure differed significantly between the two clusters (t-test with p-value .00): the organized cruisers had an average expenditure per capita of €26.8 while the independent cruisers had an expenditure of €51.

Finally, an additional t-test was conducted to verify the variance between the two clusters in relation to behavioural intentions. There was a statistically significant difference in willingness to return to Messina (p-value .00), while there was no significant difference in willingness to recommend Messina (p-value .191).

Discussion

The explorative factor analysis shows the latent factors that shape onshore satisfaction. Further, the study provides information about the socio-demographic characteristics of respondents (education and nationality) and trip-related characteristics (length of stay and trip motivation) that can moderate cruise passengers' satisfaction. Moreover, the key factor that distinguishes the clusters seems to expenditure on the onshore excursion (€65 *vs* €28).

Specifically, cruise passengers who experienced an organized tour are more satisfied with the port-related facilities and the length of stay at the destination. This cluster consists of higher-spending passengers (€51 per capita), foreigners and well educated people who travel to visit different cities, so that this cluster could be considered more demanding (Gargano & Grasso, 2016). In fact, although guided tours give opportunities for shopping and spending more money (Parola et al., 2014), this group had a low level of satisfaction with the onshore shopping experience and tourist services in general. The organized cruisers showed little willingness to return to the destination. Tourism studies have commonly found a correlation between satisfaction and behavioural intentions (Bigne et al., 2001; Prayag, 2009; Yoon & Uysal, 2005), so in this case the low level of satisfaction on the most influential factors has a negative effect on the likelihood of returning to the destination.

On the other hand, cruise passengers who experience the destination in an independent way (e. g. without buying any type of organized tour) were Italian passengers who travelled because of the low price; they tended to be high-school educated, have a lower annual income (<25k), to spend little time at the destination, to have a low expenditure per capita at the destination (€26.8) and a lower expenditure on guided tours (€28). This cluster consists of passengers who are not so demanding. In fact, they had a high level of satisfaction on the key factors, probably because they experienced the city simply by walking and also a medium-high level of perceived personal security, being Italian and consequently familiar with their surroundings. They did, though, have low levels of satisfaction with the port and welcoming services, perhaps related to a lack of information points. They had an intention to return to the destination, being mostly satisfied with the overall destination experience (Brida et al., 2013). There was no significant difference between clusters in terms of intention to recommend. These findings are well supported by the recent study of Gargano and Grasso (2016) on the same destination Messina. In fact, the authors showed that people who perceived a high level of general satisfaction, foreigners with spent more hours in destination had a higher expenditure.

Conclusion and implications

This empirical study provided a better understanding of the cruise tourists in Messina, in terms of their trip motivations and behaviours at the destination. The sample comprised 419 cruise ship passengers who had disembarked at the port of Messina between March and April 2013 for a short excursion. The study contributes to knowledge on cruise passengers' behaviour at destinations by analysing their socio-demographic characteristics and the trip characteristics (length of stay and trip motivation), their perceived satisfaction with key factors of their inland experience and their behavioural intentions. The study includes an original segmentation approach based on satisfaction, which delineated two groups: independent cruisers (people who experience the destination on their own) and organized cruisers (people who enjoy the destination via an excursion package). Specifically, our study revealed that cruise passengers visiting the destination through a guided tour tend to spend more money and are more inclined both to return to and to promote the destination. This study found that perceived personal security and the aesthetic perception of the city significantly were correlated with the likelihood of returning to and recommending Messina (Brida et al., 2012c, 2014), while the level of satisfaction with the shopping experience was correlated only with the intent to recommend Messina.

Aside from its theoretical contribution, this study is relevant to destination marketing and policy making. First, our findings show that "independent cruisers" and "organized cruisers" have different needs, perceptions and expenditure patterns; this suggests they should be targeted with specific marketing activities. For example, passengers experiencing the city by themselves (i.e. not on a tour) could be provided with a destination-specific mobile app to assist them while in the town, and thus increase both their expenditure and their satisfaction with the visit, which in turn should stimulate their intention to return and to recommend the destination to others. Further, an effort should be done by destination marketers and policy makers to create alternative tours and entertainments for cruise passengers visiting the city at the weekend (when many of the shops and attractions are closed) so that they can be stimulated to spend more and to be more satisfied with their visit; destination marketers and policy makers could also persuade cruise line companies to extend the length of stay in the destination (Brida et al., 2013). Generally speaking, it is also important to underline that when many shops and attractions are closed, few people tend to be around the city, so cruise passengers might feel unsafe and/or bored; this could, in turn, negatively affect their satisfaction and behavioural intentions.

Although this study helps to deepen existing knowledge on cruise passengers' behaviour and proposes some implications for practitioners, it does have limitations. Firstly, the study is highly site-specific, and findings cannot be generalized. Secondly, the limited period of observation did not allow us to provide a complete picture of the cruise passengers' behaviour at the city of Messina; for this reason, it should be noted that our findings describe the cruise phenomenon in the city just partially. Future studies should be done in order to collect data across the whole of the cruise season, so that policy makers and destination marketers can be provided with more detailed knowledge.

Disclosure statement

No potential conflict of interest was reported by the authors.

ORCID

Annarita Sorrentino (iD) http://orcid.org/0000-0002-5245-1407
Marcello Risitano (iD) http://orcid.org/0000-0001-9579-5931
Giacomo Del Chiappa (iD) http://orcid.org/0000-0003-4318-0462
Tindara Abbate (iD) http://orcid.org/0000-0003-3706-5206

References

Andriotis, K., & Agiomirgianakis, G. (2010). Cruise visitors' experience in a Mediterranean port of call. *International Journal of Tourism Research*, *12*(4), 390–404.

Bigne, E., Sanchez, M. I., & Sanchez, J. (2001). Tourism image, evaluation variables and after purchase behavior: Inter-relationship. *Tourism Management*, *22*(6), 607–616.

Braun, B. M., Xander, J. A., & White, K. R. (2002). The impact of the cruise industry on a region's economy: A case study of Port Canaveral, Florida. *Tourism Economics*, *8*(3), 281–288.

Brida, J. G., Bukstein, D., Garrido, N., & Tealde, E. (2012a). Cruise passengers' expenditure in the Caribbean port of call of Cartagena de Indias: A cross-section data analysis. *Tourism Economics*, *18*(2), 431–447.

Brida, J. G., Pulina, M., Riaño, E., & Aguirre, S. Z. (2013). Cruise passengers in a homeport: A market analysis. *Tourism Geographies*, *15*(1), 68–87.

Brida, J. G., Pulina, M., Riaño, E., & Zapata-Aguirre, S. (2012b). Cruise passengers' experience embarking in a Caribbean home port. The case study of Cartagena de Indias. *Ocean & Coastal Management*, *55*, 135–145.

Brida, J. G., Pulina, M., Riaño, E., & Zapata-Aguirre, S. (2012c). Cruise visitors' intention to return as land tourists and to recommend a visited destination. *Anatolia: an International Journal of Tourism and Hospitality Research*, *23*(3), 395–412.

Brida, J. G., Scuderi, R., & Seijas, M. N. (2014). Segmenting Cruise passengers visiting Uruguay: A factor–cluster analysis. *International Journal of Tourism Research*, *16*(3), 209–222.

Brida, J. G., & Zapata, S. (2010). Cruise tourism: Economic, socio-cultural and environmental impacts. *International Journal of Leisure and Tourism Marketing*, *1*(3), 205–226.

Caliński, T., & Harabasz, J. (1974). A dendrite method for cluster analysis. *Communications in Statistics-Theory and Methods*, *3*(1), 1–27.

Cattell, R. B., & Vogelmann, S. (1977). A comprehensive trial of the scree and KG criteria for determining the number of factors. *Multivariate Behavioral Research*, *12*(3), 289–325.

Chase, G., & Alon, I. (2002). Evaluating the economic impact of cruise tourism: A case study of Barbados. *Anatolia*, *13*(1), 5–18.

De Cantis, S., Ferrante, M., Kahani, A., & Shoval, N. (2016). Cruise passengers' behavior at the destination: Investigation using GPS technology. *Tourism Management*, *52*(1), 133–150.

Gabe, T. M., Lynch, C. P., & McConnon, J. C. (2006). Likelihood of cruise ship passenger return to a visited port: The case of Bar Harbor, Maine. *Journal of Travel Research*, *44*(3), 281–287.

Gargano, R., & Grasso, F. (2016). Cruise passengers' expenditure in the Messina port: A mixture regression approach. *Journal of International Studies*, *9*(2), 158–169.

Hair, J. F., Anderson, R. E., Tatham, R., & Black, W. C. (1984). *Multivariate data analysis with readings*. Indianapolis, IN: Macmillan Pub.

Henthorne, T. L. (2000). An analysis of expenditures by cruise ship passengers in Jamaica. *Journal of Travel Research*, 38(3), 246–250.

Horn, J. L. (1965). A rationale and test for the number of factors in factor analysis. *Psychometrika*, 30(2), 179–185.

Italian Cruise Watch 2016 annual report. (2016) (Ed.), Venice: Risposte Turismo for Italian Cruise Day.

McKee, D. L., & Chase, G. L. (2003). The economic impact of cruise tourism on Jamaica. *Journal of Tourism Studies*, 14(2), 16–22.

Med Cruise Annual Report. (2016). *Med Cruise activities in MedCruise ports statistics*. Piraeus, MedCruise Association.

Observatory on Tourism on European Islands (OTIE) 2009. Cruise tourism effects on The Mediterranean islands' economies. Retrieved June 20, 2011, from http://www.otie.org/it/studi-ricerche.xhtml

Ozturk, U. A., & Gogtas, H. (2016). Destination attributes, satisfaction, and the cruise visitor's intent to revisit and recommend. *Tourism Geographies*, 18(2), 194–212.

Parola, F., Satta, G., Penco, L., & Persico, L. (2014). Destination satisfaction and cruiser behaviour: The moderating effect of excursion package. *Research in Transportation Business & Management*, 13(3), 53–64.

Prayag, G. (2009). Tourists' evaluations of destination image, satisfaction, and future behavioral intentions—The case of Mauritius. *Journal of Travel & Tourism Marketing*, 26(8), 836–853.

Satta, G., Parola, F., Penco, L., & Persico, L. (2015). Word of mouth and satisfaction in cruise port destinations. *Tourism Geographies*, 17(1), 54–75.

Yoon, Y., & Uysal, M. (2005). An examination of the effects of motivation and satisfaction on destination loyalty: A structural model. *Tourism Management*, 26(1), 45–56.

Wine tourism in Mexico: an initial exploration

Gerardo Novo, Maribel Osorio and Sergio Sotomayor

ABSTRACT

In the 1980s, the wine industry in Mexico began to define its own identity, and by the end of the 1990s wine regions started to experience the attraction of their first visitors. This fact changed the producers' perspective and enhanced the definition of products and experiences associated with tourism. This paper seeks to present an overview of the current state of the wine tourism industry in Mexico, while analyzing the conditions for its emergence and growth based on a three-stage tourism model proposed by Carmichael and Senese. The development of new wine regions, the emergence of wineries and the growing interest in the food-related tourism make the wine tourism sector a promising activity in Mexico.

Introduction

Despite the fact that Mexico has a long history in wine production, which dates back to the 16th century, it has just been in the last three decades that wine tourism, has begun to consolidate itself as a tourism model with great growth potential in different areas of the country. The development of this form of tourism is still in its early stages due to the enormous potential and the boom that has experienced in just three main regions, where it has become a major driver for regional economies. The cultivation of vines for wine production, *vitis vinifera*, in the American Continent has its records back in the 16th century; it is a well-known fact that it was in Coahuila, in the northern region of the current Mexican territory, where the first vineyard of America was founded. In the region known as Valle de Parras, north of the Mexican territory, the European colonizers recognized appropriate conditions to grow vines, the evidence was the existence of American wild vines. Thus, through a grant of land the hacienda de San Lorenzo appeared in 1597, which would be the antecedent of the current Casa Madero (Corona, 2011). The historical significance of hacienda San Lorenzo is that it was the first winery created for commercial purposes, not religious or home consumption (Cerón, Faesler, & Calderwood, 2003).

Subsequently, in the 18th century, growing vines started, in the northern area of the territory, currently the state of Baja California, which nowadays produces 90% of the Mexican wine. It was by the end of the 20th century, when wine production in Mexico began to emerge as an industry with a clear vision of making high-quality products. The trade openness of Mexico in the 1980's forced the national wine industry to respond to the challenges imposed by the entry of Mexico to GATT in 1986. A key factor was also the participation of enologists, such as Camilo Magoni, Francisco Rodriguez Gonzalez, Victor Torres Alegre and Hugo D'Acosta. All of them recognized specialists, whose contribution to Mexican enology has been recognized.

The International Organization of Vine and Wine (OIV) (2017), according to 2017 figures, Mexico allocates 32,000 ha to the cultivation of vine and it is estimated that domestic consumption is around 89.5 million litres, which is equivalent to a per capita consumption of .75 ml. which locates Mexico in the 35th place. A remarkable fact is that the consumption has increased by 184% since the year 2000. Exports have doubled since the year 2007. On the other hand, exports have quadrupled since the year 2000. Therefore, the wine and enotourism are in a clear growth stage, this boom could not be understood without the existence of a market, interested and willing to consume, as well as a wide range of associated experiences.

In this century, Mexican wineries have identified in wine tourism an accurate way of increasing their participation in the wine market. Clearly, tourists represent a key component in order to increase the profits of wine consumption and the practice of other activities offered at the facilities of wineries. The development of wine tourism in Mexico cannot be understood without the initiative of wine industry, which transformed its agricultural area and redeveloped it as a place to receive visitors. The opening of vineyards to tourism in the 90's and especially in the 21st century meant a change in the proposal that led to the conversion and adaptation of productive fields into multifunctional spaces to accommodate the reception of visitors. This fact led to greater flows of visitors and, of course, has significantly contributed to increase domestic wine consumption.

The neoliberal policy established by the Mexican government in the mid 1980s, which resulted in trade openness, forced producers to make improvements in production processes, higher quality inputs and train personnel in charge of production of both grapes and wine, as well as marketing. The above-mentioned specialization has led, to the emergence and proliferation of small wineries of low production, but with sufficient quality to break into the market and position themselves strategically on the routes of wine or wine producing regions. Over the years, investment and development in those states that had traditionally been grape producers, in many cases used for the manufacture of brandy, began to revert to produce wines with their own labels also, foster visits to vineyards and wine cellars to participate in the activities scheduled throughout the year.

The dawn of the current century witnessed how little by little it started to be a phenomenon of "discovery" of wine tourism as a highly rewarding experience that could be supplemented as part of the visits to towns or regions close to the large Mexican cities like Tijuana, Monterrey, Mexico City and Querétaro. The first vineyards established at the end of the last century began to conform wine producing regions and subsequently led to the consolidation of gastronomic and thematic routes. The Wine Route in Baja California and the Route of Art, Wine and Cheese in Querétaro appeared. An important fact, that has catalyzed the development of this type of trips, is the relative ease that wine tourism has to generate productive chaining and value based on gastronomic and wine production. All of the previously mentioned has made it possible to link it with dozens of other activities, which as a whole, have led to the rapid growth of the supply intended for different consumer segments. Thus, to those activities of traditional and historical destinations, organization of festivals, wine tastings, competitions, exhibitions and other events related to wine culture were added. All this, enhanced by a considerable increase in the emergence of specialized publications in gastronomy, wine and tourism magazines that promote wine consumption.

Additionally, local authorities and the private sector have encouraged marketing and promotional strategies in mass media and social networks to position destinations and regions of Mexico as gastronomic destinations and particularly as wine producers. Communication strategies have been articulated through a journalistic and advertising discourse, which in addition to the consumption of popular culture products, have contributed to the construction of a popular consciousness of wine tourism, which connotes social prestige, where the wine tourist can become a "connoisseur" and whose travel experience is equipped with elements that represent the good living.

In recent years, Mexican wine seeks to be internationally recognized. An advantage, among other aspects, is the prestige of Mexican cuisine, considered as intangible cultural heritage of humanity by UNESCO in 2010 and it has also been considered as a self-defined feature of Mexican culture, product of its history and cultural diversity.

Literature review

The emergence of wine tourism as a modality and its study have increased research in the area and the appearance of academic journals. According to Duran, Del Río, and Álvarez (2016) the first article focused on wine tourism, was written in 1984, but it has been in the last five years when more than 60% of the present papers have been published in platforms of scientific information as Web of Science and Scopus, also is notorious the greater presence of papers from Australia, United States, Spain and Canada. Scientific literature on wine tourism has been classified according to Carlsen and Charters (2006) in five thematic groupings: (i) wine tourism culture and heritage, (ii) wine tourism business; (iii) wine tourism marketing; (iv) wine tourists and (v) wine tourism systems.

For Mitchell and Hall (2006) wine tourism literature can be defined into seven groups: Wine tourism product; Wine tourism and regional development, Quantification on demand; Segmentation of wine tourists; Visitor´s behaviour; Nature of visit to wineries; Food safety and wine tourism. Based on these two classifications, a non exhaustive but general overview of academic literature related to wine tourism can be described and notice a lack of information about wine tourism development in Mexico.

A review of the literature shows that one of the most remarkable facts about wine tourism is that it has been seen as a mechanism for economic growth and specially recognized by vine producers as a resource for developing agricultural complementary activities and promote local and regional development (Boyne, Hall, & Williams, 2012; Carmichael & Senese, 2012; Martinez & Morales, 2016; Medina, 2011). Therefore, tourism has had a positive effect on wine producing regions and sustainable regional development (Duarte & Liu, 2012; Howley & van Westering, 2008; Sparks & Malady, 2006). Beyond economic development, wine tourism has shown its capacity to provide a distinctive image destination associated to local agricultural production and gastronomy as well as an attraction that encourages visiting destinations (Fronchot, 2012; Valderrama, Meraz, Velázquez, & Flores, 2012). Gastronomy plays an important role in the way tourist seek and experience the destination (Hjalager & Richards, 2002; Jeambey, 2016; Kivela & Crotts, 2006; López-Guzman, Rodríguez-García, & Vieira-Rodríguez, 2013).

From a marketing perspective, specifically tourism marketing destination, research has focused on finding strategies that allow regions and vineyards to establish competitive advantages in their environment by taking advantage of their conditions such as location, quality of the visit, scenic beauty, landscape, hosts' attitude, and environment among other aspects (Barber, Donovan, & Dodd, 2008; Bruwer & Alant, 2009; Carlsen & Charters, 2006; Hashimoto & Telfer, 2012). In this sense, the study of demand has led to a better understanding of the reasons for travelling and evaluation of experiences in the visit. The result has given rise to frames of explanation to study the different motivations that drive wine tourists and propose strategies for segmentation according to market niches (Baird, Hall, & Castka, 2018; Carmichael, 2005; Mitchell, Hall, & McIntosh, 2002; Molina, Gomez, González-Díaz, & Esteban, 2015; Nella & Christou, 2014; Pratt, 2014). Factors as attributes of a winery, themes and activities, education and novelty contribute to a memorable wine-tasting experience according to Saayman & van der Merwe (2015).

The study of wine tourism in Mexico, despite the fact that the issue has become relevant in the last 20 years, it is still incipient. Most of the research focuses on tourism supply. Literature review shows that research has focused geographically in three major regions: Baja California, north of Mexico; Querétaro, in the central region of the country and Coahuila. These are the three major wine producing areas of the country; they are also the ones that concentrate the largest number of visitors.

A significant proportion of the *corpus* is empirical research from a marketing approach intending to analyze the competitiveness and seek opportunities in the market (Alpizar & Maldonado, 2009; Meraz & Maldonado, 2016; Meraz & Ruiz, 2016; Quiñones, Bringas, & Barrios., 2011; Ruiz, Martínez, Verján, & Valderrama, 2011; Velásquez, 2007). One of the reasons that encouraged the making of the present study was the scarceness of information about the current state of wine tourism in Mexico. While it is true that there has been a growth in the consumption of wine and the emergence of new vineyards, wine cellars and labels, a study to have a general idea of status of this type of tourism has not been addressed in a comprehensive manner. This implies that, as a tourism phenomenon, it may not be sufficiently described or quantified in terms of volume, affluence, and economic benefit to determine the impact both in the localities and regions where it is developed as well as their socio-economic and environmental impacts. The lack of statistics and systematic study of wine tourism evolution regarding these particular issues decreases the possibility of analysis and withholds the possibility of deepening in aspects related to supply and demand.

Methodology

Having in mind the contribution to a better understanding of wine tourism in Mexico, one of the main purposes of this research was to locate firstly wineries open to the public offering wine tourism activities. This is important to highlight, because it constitute one of the first attempts to identify wineries focused on tourism demand in Mexico. Despite the growing production and consume of Mexican wine, not all the wineries are able to receive visitors. That is why the intention to identify wineries focused on producing and tourism.

A research instrument was designed, for the collection of data, to identify, firstly, the number and geographical location of commercial establishments devoted to wine production and focused on tourism. The collection of data was carried out approximately during six months, based on a documentary search in travel guides, promotional brochures of enological routes, wine tasters guides, specialized publications, academic articles and websites of wineries and tourism promotion of wine producing states, which allowed in a first phase to make a general list of wineries. Additionally, phone calls were made to Tourism offices in order to identify wine tourism as a product considered as real local attraction and get further information about existence of wineries and routes.

The research only considered as a positive result when personal communication was established with owners or employees through phone calls or e-mails to confirm the information collected. From a total of 199 wineries found, only in 135 cases was possible to confirm the existence of tourism activities. In case of small wineries owners or relatives highly involved used to talk about the vineyards or cellars. In the case of medium and big wineries in a few cases was possible to talk directly with the owner, so managers or public relation personal attended the interview. Respondents were considered always they were authorized or involved with the business.

Research was focused on the relationship of wine producing business with tourism, for that purpose, a short questionnaire was developed to identify the characteristics of the vineyard. A few questions were included in order to confirm the existence of the winery, opening date, activities offered to visitors, webpage and contact channels for further information. Because of the distance and the expensive cost of travelling along the country, it was not possible to interview face-to-face, so communication with respondents was considered through this via.

Data collected was organized in order to present the first findings, which made it possible to draw up an inventory of Mexican wineries, their geographical distribution and their relation with tourism.

Besides proposing a tourism winery inventory, the second phase of the research was based in a three-stage tourism model developed by Carmichael and Senese. This was considered as a reference and used to identify stages of development in wine tourism Mexican regions. Carmichael and Senese (2012, p. 175) suggest stage model provide a start in the development of a framework and in the search for analytic tools to examine the relative ability to cope with various forms of tourism development. The proposed model outlines the importance of three factors in destination development: supply, users and external forces as social, political, economic, and cultural environments. The model distinguishes three stages, in broad outline, described below:

Stage 1 *(e1)* **Winery Independence**:	Stage 2 *(e2)* **Wine Tourism Development:**	Stage 3 *(e3)* **Wine Tourism Integration:**
An initial phase in which optimum physical conditions for the cultivation of vine and production begins through independent producers. At this stage, there is no integration or connection between producers to generate synergies.	The development of wine tourism begins; there are networks between some wineries, other attractions and services. A wine route is developed, the flows of tourists move through designed tours and paths to offer themed tours. The tourist supply of enotourism starts to be identified, joint promotion is launched and special events and shows are developed. A brand identity starts to be projected and begins to emerge as a wine *cluster*.	It is characterized by a more complex tourism product through the alliance of wineries. Joint actions in marketing increase, organization of festivals, greater flow of information and travellers among business. Greater involvement of public and private entities.

Source: Adapted from Carmichael and Senese (2012)
Permission obtained from Springer Nature.

The three-stages tourism model was applied, unfortunately gathered information was considered only in two aspects: analysis of supply and external forces, two of the factors suggested by Carmichael and Senese in the tourism model. Lack of statistics and demand characteristics in these entities prevented a better knowledge of visitors and its behaviour.

Results

In agreement with the Department of Agriculture, Livestock, Rural Development, Fishery and Food (Secretaría de Agricultura, Ganadería, Desarrollo Rural, Pesca y Alimentación, SAGARPA), the federal agency of the Mexican Government, there are 14 states in the country that produce wine. However, in this work only nine states that are clearly producers of *vitis vinifera*: Baja California, Coahuila, Chihuahua, Nuevo León, Queretaro, Guanajuato, San Luis Potosí, Aguascalientes and Zacatecas were identified (see Figure 1).

Three decades ago, the few existing Mexican vineyards were mostly agricultural agribusiness and in minimum extent were open spaces for visitors and consumers eager to know the wine production process. Vineyards in Baja Californian, for example, started to open their celebrations of harvest to the public in 1990.

The current scenario is completely different, nowadays, nearly 200 wineries are registered, 135 out of those 200 are open to the public and offer more than 50 different activities ranging from tours and wine tastings to massive concerts. The range of activities may have little or no relation with viticulture and winemaking, but it attracts visitors and generates profits to winemakers, in addition to wine sales.

Some states started to produce *vitis vinifera* and others have reoriented their production and have dared to produce their own labels. This is important because the wine producing states of the centre and north of Mexico are not located in the world-famous strip of wine where vineyards of Baja California are located.

For the purposes of this analysis, three types of Mexican states dedicated to wine production are distinguished:

(A) **Traditional producer states** and that, up to date, maintain high production in quantity and quality: Coahuila and Baja California, which have produced wine for more than a century and continue to maintain a significant production.
(B) **Developing producing states**: Aguascalientes, Chihuahua, Guanajuato, Queretaro, San Luis Potosi and Zacatecas. Entities that have experienced ups and downs in the production, they have historically grown grapes for wine and brandy. Nowadays, these entities are engaged in the production of grapes and wines. This group includes Sonora, a state that has traditionally been a grape producer and is now working in the production of their own labels.

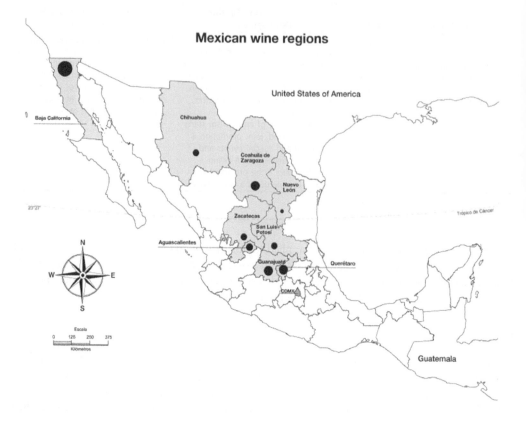

Figure 1. Mexican wine regions.

(C) **Emerging producer states**: Entities currently considered as non-producers and that have begun to produce wine recently or are making plans to produce it soon, will be incorporated into the existing supply. This group includes Nuevo León, Hidalgo and Puebla. These last two states are already experimenting with some varieties and have announced projects that will be up and running in a couple of years.

In the opinion of Cerón et al (2003), the Mexican wine is experiencing a period of "revival" within the new world wines. At the same time, wineries are opening spaces to deepen understanding, *in situ*, about grape and wine production associated with different experiences and activities.

Another important factor that has driven the development of wine tourism in Mexico is the fact that this modality has idealized the experience of approaching to production and enjoyment of wine. Its consumption is the answer to a global trend associated with ideologies of good living styles and healthy practices. Overall, this is a form of cultural tourism that brings knowledge and pleasant experiences through gastronomy.

Based on Carmichael and Senese's (2012) model a typology of wine tourism in Mexico is proposed in accordance with the phase of development in which the different states are (see Figure 2).

According to the degree of development, three types of Mexican enotourism model were found and summarized as follows considering supply:

Stage 1 *(e1)* Winery Independence:
5 states: Aguascalientes, Zacatecas, SLP, Chihuahua, Nuevo Leon.
Total of wine cellars: 32
Open wine cellars: 14

State	Wineries	Wineries open to the public	Stage of development
Baja California	107	87	**e3**
Querétaro	28	16	e2
Guanajuato	16	9	e2
Coahuila	16	9	e2
Aguascalientes	9	5	e1
Chihuahua	8	6	e1
Zacatecas	7	1	e1
San Luis Potosí	7	1	e1
Nuevo León	1	1	e1
Total	199	135	

Figure 2. Staged of development based on Carmichael and Senese (2012).

These five entities have appropriate conditions for the cultivation of vine and they have a business culture that can quickly turn the wine industry into a major regional economic driver. These states have traditionally been considered as producers, except Nuevo Leon. The five states which organize harvest and the Wine Festival in San Luis Potosi must be highlighted due to the fact that it began to attract tourists' attention from nearby entities. None of the entities has established routes so far, although there are associations of producers. Additionally, vineyards have already been integrated to the image and tourism promotion.

Stage 2 *(e2)* **Wine Tourism Development**:

3 States: Queretaro, Guanajuato, Coahuila

Total of wine cellars: 60

Open Wine cellars: 34

Queretaro and Guanajuato are characterized particularly by the rapid growth of their production plant and the marketing strategies they are using to position themselves as wine-producing regions. The three states have traditionally been producers and have a business culture that has made the industrial development easier in their territory. There are formal channels of communication and organization among producers, which has allowed in all three cases, to design and to build a wine route that takes flows of tourists between towns, businesses and other attractions.

The joint promotion between authorities and individuals allows a projection of enotourism supply in addition to activities that include the participation of various businesses. The making of events and shows is common throughout the year as harvests, festivals, concerts, art markets, competitions, wine tastings and themed dinners, among others. The flow of visitors is constant and these destinations have the capacity to attract tourists from all around the region. Wine cellars and wineries offer free tours and are marketed through strategic alliances. Coahuila and Queretaro, mainly, have managed to build an identity as wine producers and a wine *cluster* starts to emerge in each of these entities.

Stage 3 *(e3)* **Wine Tourism Integration**

1 State: Baja California

Total of wineries: 107

Open wine cellars: 87

This is the best-positioned and articulated model for enotourism in Mexico. Despite its weaknesses and opportunities, it is considered a tourist product that has reached its consolidation through the integration of wineries and specialized services in the so-called Wine Route, it has a

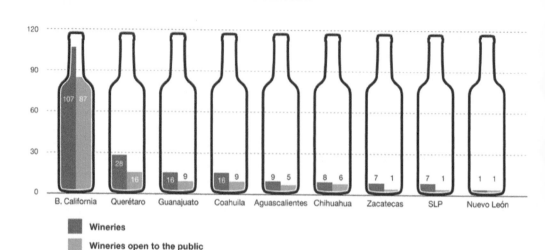

Figure 3. Wineries and wineries open to the public.

supply of high-quality service, as well as high involvement of public and private entities for the implementation of activities and joint strategies for promotion and marketing. In the last 15 years, there has been a considerable increase in the making of festivals, contests, themed dinners, concerts and other activities. The region has been a centre of attraction for restaurants, homebrew beer production and renowned chefs. One of the advantages is its positioning as the best wine region of the country.

Therefore, three stages of development are identified, according to the stage model proposed by Carmichael and Senese used for the analysis. These three types of wine tourism development in Mexico render account of its heterogeneity and the possibilities of development in the future. In time of completion of this research, 199 established wineries were identified in Mexico; SAGARPA claims that there are 207. As can be seen, the largest concentration of these businesses are located in the region of Baja California with almost a 64% of the total business. In this sense, Baja California keeps the leadership in production; nine out of every 10 Mexican wines are produced there. On the other hand, the entity also maintains a leadership in quality, as the region gets the best scores, according to the guidelines of wine tasters of Bodenstedt (2016) and Gerschmann (2017), both recognized opinion leaders in enological practices (see Figure 3).

Conclusion and implications

Despite the growth of enotourism in Mexico in the last 30 years, its development is still incipient, especially when compared to other forms of travelling practiced in the country and to other places that have promoted it for decades. On the other hand, it is observed that the development of this form of tourism is presented with marked differences between regions; this is why their development is not homogeneous. In general terms, the development of wine tourism in Mexico can be understood essentially due to the following factors considering social, political and cultural environments:

- Structural changes in wine production caused by the opening up of trade, which led to a transformation of the wine industry that brought increased investment, innovation and design of new wines with higher quality.

- Greater competition in the market in which a wide range of wine varietals, assemblies and author wines began to be offered in order to differentiate and position themselves in the taste and preference of traditional segments and new consumers.
- The view of tourism as an opportunity to increase sales, diversify the market and generate a culture of wine.
- The conversion of rural and agricultural space in a multifunctional space oriented to leisure and its ability to adapt to a changing environment.
- The socialization of a symbolism of wine, able of pushing up a significant tourist demand, associated to good living, gastronomic culture, health, well-being and search for new experiences.

We can also say that the development of wine tourism in Mexico is characterized by:

- A marked heterogeneity of its supply, according to the model of analysis used (Carmichael & Senese, 2012), regions with traits of the three stages of development are distinguished: (e1) Winery independence, (e2) Wine Tourism Development, and Wine Tourism Integration (e3).
- A process of restructuring of the gastronomic experience of consumption based on wines and other local products through touristic practice, which has boomed the last 20 years.
- The emergence of small wine cellars, exhibition centres, museums, shops and other establishments to show the processes of production and elaboration of wine and become sales channels.
- A gradual transition from wine cellars to wine growing having in mind the quality control throughout the whole process.
- The progressive conversion of the productive plant in wine production with a strong orientation towards the tourist market.
- The creation and design of routes, thematic events such as festivals, parties and fairs, among others, based on the local gastronomic supply which has allowed and encouraged productive and valuable chaining between tourist offer and complementary offer of regions.
- The inclusion of wine tourism, as a tourist product, in the strategies of promotion and particularly in the tourist image projected by the states and regions of Mexico.

In spite of the positive factors that illustrate the important development that wine tourism is taking in Mexico, this Latin American country faces significant challenges that have decelerated its growth. Business owners are aware of the high investment that wine production represents and its slow rate of return. Additionally, the high cost of Mexican wines due to transfer of taxes to consumers and they have to cope with strong competition with foreign wines, especially those that pay low import tariffs or have subsidies in production.

While it might be thought that the segments that practice this type of tourism are conformed by flows of gastronomic tourists, it is true that in many cases, the supply of Mexican vineyards is not confined to wine production activities, but has been extended to artistic or festive activities in which wine becomes a complement and not the categorical element of the visit, which allows different segments of visitors to rise, who do not necessarily have an interest in the knowledge and enjoyment of wine, but in pure hedonism.

If the 1980s were the breaking point for Mexican wines, the beginning of the 21st century represents that moment for enotourism in Mexico. From this century Mexican vineyards ceased to be a purely agricultural space to become a multifunctional space in which activities, directly related to winemaking, take place but also other that are completely far from it and that respond more to the diversification and entertainment strategies of wineries.

That is how, vineyard went from being an agricultural space to be a forum for shows, which turns the "show" into the main reason of visit and not wine itself. This is important because it presents a distinction between segments interested in the knowledge and consumption of wine and other segments whose central theme is only leisure and entertainment.

Enotourism in Mexico is at an early stage in the process of growth and expansion. It is still an incipient model, but with a lot of potential. The analysis shows that most of the states are at a first phase of development and that there is a high concentration principally in three states: Baja California, Queretaro and Coahuila.

Another important fact is that the creation of new establishments and vineyards is being planned to attract flows of tourists, unlike the first wineries that only thought of producing wine.

The development of wine tourism in Mexico is due to an increase in the consumption of this beverage whose imagery is associated with practices and healthy habits as it is part of the Mediterranean diet, as a sign of distinction, good taste, culture and knowledge.

The different ways of travelling, the seek for new experiences, the diversification of supply, the increase in the number of tourists and the exhaustion of traditional mass tourism also contribute to promoting this type of tourism. Its growth in years to come will be reflected in the extent in which Mexican wine producers recognize that tourism is a viable option to increase the consumption of their products.

Mexico has high potential to become one of the main enology-and-food related destinations in the world, its diversity and cultural richness drive it and hold it. The different regions that are currently in the process of development must be consolidated, such task is not an easy one because it requires a high economic investment, maintain quality standards that distinguish the business from the rivals and avoid saturation in a market that has shown signs of rapid expansion. On the other hand, public policies are needed to foster development of local regions, wine tourism represents a means to do so. Undoubtedly, it is a matter of care, knowledge, passion and time, just as fine wines.

Disclosure statement

No potential conflict of interest was reported by the authors.

References

Alpizar, V., & Maldonado, M. (2009). Integración de la Ruta del Vino en Querétaro un producto innovador [Wine route integration at Queretaro innovative product]. *Quivera, 11*(2), 97–109.

Baird, T., Hall, M., & Castka, P. (2018). New Zealand winegrowers attitudes and behaviours towards wine tourism and sustainable winegrowing. *Sustainability, 10*(3), 797–799.

Barber, N., Donovan, J., & Dodd, T. (2008). Differences in tourism marketing.: Strategies between wineries base on size and location. *Journal of Travel and Tourism Marketing, 25*(1), 43–57.

Bodenstedt, A. (2016). *Guía de Vinos Mexicanos.* Artboden: Mexican Wine Guide.

Boyne, S., Hall, D., & Williams, F. (2012). Policy, support and promotion for food-related tourism iniatives: A marketing approach to regional development in wine, food and tourism marketing. *Journal of Travel and Tourism Marketing, 14*(3/4), 131–154.

Bruwer, J., & Alant, K. (2009). The hedonic nature of wine tourism consumption: An experiential view. *International Journal of Wine Business Research, 21*(3), 235–257.

Carlsen, J., & Charters, S. (Eds.). (2006). Global wine tourism. In *Research, management and marketing*. Cambridge, MA: CABI.

Carmichael, B. (2005). Understanding the wine tourism experience for winery visitors in the Niagara Region, Ontario, Canadá. *Tourism Geographies, 2*(3), 229–237.

Carmichael, B., & Senese, D. (2012). Competitiveness and sustainability in wine tourism regions: The application of a stage model of destination development to two Canadian wine regions. In Dougherty, P. H. (Ed.) *The geography of wine: Regions, terroir and techniques* (pp. 159–177). USA: Springer.

Cerón, R., Faesler, C., & Calderwood, M. (2003). *El vino mexicano, raíz, sarmiento y fruto. México*. [Mexican Wine, Root, Vine Shoot and Fruit] Mexico, D. F.: Revimundo.

Corona, S. (2011). Turismo y vino en la D. O. Valle de Parras. Coahuila en Medina [Tourism and wine at D. O. Valle de Parras, Coahuila]. X. F., Serrano, D, & Treserras, J. In X. F. Medina, D. Serrano, & J. Treserras (Eds.), *Turismo del vino: Análisis de casos internacionales [Wine tourism: International experiences analysis]*. Barcelona: UOC.

Duarte, A. A., & Liu, Y. (2012). Old wine region, new concept and sustainable development: Winery entrepreneur´s perceived benefits from wine tourism on Spain´s Canary Islands. *Journal of Sutainable Tourism, 20*(7), 991–1009.

Duran, A., Del Río, M. C., & Álvarez, J. (2016). Bibliometric analysis of publications on wine tourism in the databases Scopus and WoS. *European Research of Management and Business Economics, 23*(1), 8–15.

Fronchot, I. (2012). An analysis of regional positioning and its associated food images in French tourism regional brochures. *Journal of Travel and Tourism Marketing, 14*(3/4), 77–98.

Gerschman, R. (2012). *Guía de catadores del vino mexicano [Mexican wine taster´s guide]*. México: Planeta.

Hashimoto, A., & Telfer, D. (2012). Positioning an emerging wine route in the Niagara Region: Understanding the wine tourism market and its implications for marketing. *Journal of Travel and Tourism Marketing, 14*(3/4), 61–76.

Hjalager, A., & Richards, G. (2002). *Tourism and gastronomy*. New York: Routledge.

Howley, M., & van Westering, J. (2008). Developing wine tourism: A case study of the attitude of English wine producers to wine tourism. *Journal of Vacation Marketing, 14*(7–8), 86–95.

Jeambey, Z. (2016). Rutas gastronómicas y Desarrollo local: un ensayo de conceptualización en Cataluña [Gastronomic routes and local development: An essay of conceptualization in Catalonia]. *PASOS. Revista de Turismo y Patrimonio Cultural, 14*(5), 1187–1198.

Kivela, J., & Crotts, J. (2006). Tourism and gastronomy´s influence on how tourists experience destination. *Journal of Hospitality and Tourism Research, 30*, 354–377.

López-Guzman, T., Rodríguez-García, J., & Vieira-Rodríguez, A. (2013). Revisión de la Literatura Científica sobre Enoturismo en España [Review of the scientific literature on wine tourism in Spain]. *Cuadernos de Turismo, 32*, 171–188.

Martínez, A., & Morales, F. (2016). El vino como recurso turístico para el fomento del desarrollo local. Una oportunidad para las comarcas de Vinalopó (Alicante) y el altiplano Yecla-Jumilla (Murcia). [The wine, as a tourist resource for the promotion of local development. An opportunity for the region of Vinalopó (Alicante) and the highlands Yecla-Jumilla (Murcia)]. *Cuadernos de Turismo, 38*, 263–295.

Medina, X. F. (2011). Turismo del vino y desarrollo local en la región vitivinícola de Tokaj-Hegyalja (Hungría) en El turismo del vino: Experiencias internacionales [Wine tourism and local development in Tokaj-Hegylia, Hungary, in wine tourism: International experiences analysis]. In X. F. Medina, D. Serrano, & J. Treserras (Eds.). Barcelona: UOC.

Meraz, L., & Maldonado, R. (2016). Influencia de la oferta de actividades de enoturismo en la competitividad de las micro, pequeñas, medianas vinícolas de la Ruta del Vino del Valle de Guadalupe, B. C., México [Influence of wine tourism in the competitiveness of micro, small and medium-sized wineries in Guadalupe Valley, B. C. Mexico] México. *Revista Global de Negocios, 4*(1), 47–59.

Meraz, L., & Ruiz, A. (2016). El enoturismo de Baja California, México: un análisis de su oferta y comparación con la región de La Rioja, España. [Wine tourism in Baja California, Mexico: An analysis of its supply and a comparison with the wine region of La Rioja, Spain]. *Investigaciones Turísticas, 12*, 73–98.

Mitchell, R., & Hall, M. (2006). Wine Tourism Research: The State of Play. *Tourism Review International, 9*, 307–332.

Mitchell, R., Hall, M., & McIntosh, A. (2002). Wine tourism and consumer behaviour. In Hall, M., Sharples, L., Cambourne, B., & Macionis, N. (Eds.),*Wine tourism around the world. Development, management and markets* (pp. 115–135). Oxford: Elsevier.

Molina, A., Gomez, M., González-Díaz, B., & Esteban, A. (2015). Market segmentation in wine tourism: Strategies for wineries and destinations in Spain. *Journal of Wine Research, 26*(3), 192–224.

Nella, A., & Christou, E. (2014). Segmenting wine tourists on the basis of involvement with wine. *Journal of Travel and Tourism Marketing, 31*(7), 783–798.

International Organization of Vine and Wine. (2017). *2017 world vitiviniculture situation*. OIV Statistical Report on World Vitiviniculture. Paris: OIV.

Pratt, M. (2014). Four wine tourist profiles. *Academy of wine business research. 8th international conference*. Geisenhem, Germany.

Quiñones, J., Bringas, N., & Barrios., C. (2011). La Ruta del Vino de Baja California. [Baja California wine route]. In *Patrimonio Cultural y Turismo Cuadernos No 18*. México: Conaculta.

Ruiz, J. G., Martínez, O., Verján, R., & Valderrama, P. (2011). Aproximaciones al turismo enológico y sus estrategias de mercadotecnia en México [An approach to marketing strategies for wine tourism in Mexico]. *Gestión Turística, 16*, 137–155.

Saymann, M., & van der Merwe, A. (2015). Factors determining visitors´ memorable wine-testing experiences at wineries. *Anatolia: An International Journal of Tourism and Hospitality Research, 26*(3), 372–383.

Sparks, B., & Malady, J. (2006). Emerging wine tourism regions: Lessons for development in global wine tourism. In J. Carlsen & S. Chaters (Eds.), *Research, management and marketing*. Oxon: CABI.

Valderrama, J., Meraz, L., Velázquez, G., & Flores, J. C. (2012). Rutas enológicas como estrategia de posicionamiento turístico para Baja California, Mexico. [Wine routes as estrategy of tourist positioning for Baja California, Mexico]. *Global conference in business and finances proceedings, 2*. Costa Rica.

Velásquez, A. (2007). *Diseño de un modelo de sistema enoturístico para la región vitivinícola del estado de Querétaro. [Design for a wine tourism model for Queretaro region]* (Thesis). IPN, Mexico.

Tourism in the Blue Growth strategy: a model proposal

Beatriz Mayén Cañavate, Juan Andrés Bernal Conesa(iD), Antonio Juan Briones Peñalver(iD)
and Pedro Anunciação

ABSTRACT
This paper aims to be a first approximation to analyze tourism along with the concept of Blue Growth in Spain and Portugal. Therefore, the purpose of this paper is to validate a model, which relates nautical tourism to the three perspectives of Blue Growth: economic, social and environmental. The first section introduces the importance of the maritime and marine industry within the European Union. The next section analyzes the concept of Blue Growth and the different policies that have been prepared for their development, paying particular attention to tourism. The following, describes tourism in general and nautical tourism and finally establishes the methodology used for the development of the research, and conclusions as well as future lines of research.

Introduction

Blue Growth specifically focus on the next economical and marine areas as a blue energy, aquaculture, maritime tourism industry, coastal and cruisers, marine mineral resources and blue biotechnology (Lillebø, Pita, Garcia Rodrigues, Ramos, & Villasante, 2017). In this context, oceans, seas and coasts are the main motor of growth therefore, they support a wide range of human activities providing human well-being not only the population but also, a whole series of direct and indirect beneficiaries through the value chain and jobs related to the Sea sector.

Within the many aspects of the Blue Growth, the less academically developed is the tourism. Renewable energies (Rodríguez-Rodríguez, Malak, Soukissian, & Sánchez-Espinosa, 2016), fishing (Mulazzani, Trevisi, Manrique, & Malorgio, 2016), seabed mining and the Ocean and Seas planning (Frazao Santos, Domingos, Ferreira, Orbach, & Andrade, 2014; Pinto, Cruz, & Combe, 2015) have been already investigated. However, the involvement of the tourism in the Blue Growth as a source of enrichment and sustainability has not been studied extensively enough, despite of tourism have caused some environmental problems, in the future could have a negative impact in tourism itself, especially, those related to the quality of waters (Mulazzani et al., 2016). Due to all, the purpose of this paper is to validate a model through a questionnaire, which relates nautical tourism to the three perspectives of blue growth: economic, social and environmental.

Literature review

Blue economy was defined by the economist Pauli (2015) as a macroeconomic and business model oriented to respond to everyone´s basic needs with the available resources. Through this model a huge range of benefits are generated, highlighting among other things the creation of new jobs and because of that, the capital social increase with an active protection of the natural environment. The blue economy represents 5.4 million jobs and a gross added value of almost 500,000 million euro per year (European Commission, 2012). But, it could generate much more employment, if it is invested in the area and at the right time and, this is precisely what the "blue growth" of the European Commission does.

The blue growth concept was defined by the European Union (UE) as the maritime contribution to achieve the objectives of the UE in reference to sustainable development. The "blue growth" can represents a real change; tangible and positive for the economy and, thus, for all the citizens of Europe. For that reason, guidelines and legal frameworks are being provided so that, the national governments channel this growth as soon as possible, without harming the environment, so from this perspective, Blue Growth includes all economic industries related to the seas and coastal areas including tourism, fishing, navigation, mining, and biotechnology, among others (Mulazzani et al., 2016). The "blue economy" is gaining emphasis in the formulation of European policies due to the expansion of its relevance beyond traditional industries, but also to new developments that show rapid growth (Pinto et al., 2015). Therefore, the blue growth strategy of the EU allows the development of maritime activities while maintaining a high level of environmental protection.

Blue Growth strategy

On 20 February 2014, the European Commission (EC) adopted the communication entitled "A European strategy for further growth and employment in coastal and maritime tourism", which presents a new strategy to improve this type of tourism in Europe and take advantage of the potential of this promising sector. The high quality of bathing waters and the coastal and marine habitats in the virgin state have a high recreational value. The Strategy consists of three main components: Integrated maritime policy, strategy of the maritime basins and specific activities or actions, which are reflected in Table 1.

The EC has identified 14 measures that can contribute to the sustainable growth of the industry and give new impetus to European coastal regions(Anonymous, 2016). In summary, the most important ones that concern the Nautical Tourism are: (1) strive to make available coastal and maritime information; (2) promote EU tourism initiatives with promotion and communication campaigns; (3) promote a European-wide dialogue between cruise operators, ports and stakeholders in the industry; (4) support the development of transnational and interregional associations, as well as networks, business groups and smart specialization strategies; (5) evaluate, at the EU level, what is related to the qualifications of the personnel and what refers to the security teams; (6) Promote ecotourism, using the indicators of the European Environmental Management and Audit System (EMAS) and the EU Ecolabel; (7) Promote strategies for the prevention and management of waste and marine debris; (8) Encourage the diversification and integration of destinations of interest, both coastal and inland; (9) Prepare an online guide where the main funding possibilities for SMEs will be presented; and finally, (10) stimulate innovative management plans Regarding the degree of implementation of these measures, there is no up-to-date information as the 2020 horizon is expected to be completed in order to reliably analyze the result of these measures.

Differences between economy, blue growth and blue tourism

The difference is that the "Blue economy" is a macroeconomic and business model and "Blue growth" is a long-term strategy to support sustainable growth by supporting said macroeconomic model to the Maritime and Marine industry (Burgess, Clemence, McDermott, Costello, & Gaines, 2016).

Table 1. Components of the blue growth strategy.

Components	Implications or objectives	Application, measures or actions
Integrated maritime policy	Marine knowledge to improve access to information about the sea	Such access is possible through the website of the European Network of Observation and Information of the Sea, in which engineers and scientists can see what data exist about a given maritime basin and download original observations and data elaborated
	Maritime spatial planning to ensure effective and sustainable management of activities at sea	In July 2014, the European Parliament and the Council adopted a Directive to create a common framework for maritime spatial planning in Europe. Competition in the maritime space requires effective management to avoid possible conflicts and allow different activities to complement each other
	Integrated maritime surveillance so that authorities have a better appreciation of what happens at sea	The Commission recently adopted a Communication on exchanges of information on EU maritime issues that will integrate existing surveillance systems and networks and give all interested authorities access to the information they need to carry out their activities at sea
Maritime Basin Strategy	Ensure the combination of more appropriate measures in order to promote sustainable growth to take into account local climatic, oceanographic, economic, cultural and social factors in each of the maritime basins	Adriatic Sea and Ionian Sea: On 17 June 2014, the European Commission launched a new strategy for the Adriatic and Ionian regions, which focuses mainly on the opportunities of the maritime economy: blue growth, land-sea transport, energy connectivity, protection of the marine environment and promotion of sustainable tourism.
		Arctic Ocean: Avoid climate change through global agreements.
		Atlantic Ocean: The agreed measures will focus on the promotion of the tourism market, attention to the growing demand for offshore energy facilities, the improvement of education and training in traditional and emerging maritime industries and cooperation in ocean research to evaluate better the consequences of climate change.
		Baltic Sea: In May 2014, the European Commission adopted the Baltic Sea agenda for sustainable growth. It focuses on: Promoting innovation and sustainability; development of skills and qualifications, development of groupings; use existing cooperation structures and multi-sectoral dialogue. The European Commission is ready to facilitate the implementation of the Baltic Sea agenda in cooperation with stakeholders.
		Black Sea: The Black Sea Synergy, launched by the EU, is a regional cooperation initiative with the Black Sea. It was designed as a flexible framework to ensure greater coherence and political orientation, while at the same time inviting a more integrated approach.
		Mediterranean Sea: Although the Mediterranean Sea bathes more than 20 countries, much of its waters are outside of national jurisdictions. Therefore, cooperation is essential to: (1) manage maritime activities, (2) protect the marine environment and maritime heritage, (3) prevent and combat pollution, (4) improve maritime safety, (5) promote blue growth and the creation of jobs. In the Mediterranean, the PMI focuses on enhancing cooperation and governance, as well as fostering sustainable growth.
		North Sea: In September 2013, the European Parliament adopted a regional strategy for the North Sea region aimed at supporting inter-sectoral maritime cooperation in the North Sea Region through a bottom-up process involving stakeholders in financing, space and resource management, environmental issues and innovation

(Continued)

Table 1. (Continued).

Components		Implications or objectives	Application, measures or actions
Specific activities	Aquaculture		The aquaculture industry is to be promoted through the reform of the common fisheries policy and in 2013, strategic guidelines were published which present common priorities and general objectives at EU level, and according to these the Commission and the EU countries collaborate to contribute to the increase of production and the competitiveness of the industry.
	Marine Biotechnology		The so-called blue biotechnology deals with the exploration and exploitation of marine organisms in order to create new products. The exploration of the biodiversity of the sea can allow us to develop new pharmaceutical products or industrial enzymes that can withstand extreme conditions and, therefore, suppose a high economic value. Underwater technology allows us to explore the sea and proceed with genetic sequencing to analyze its living organisms.
	Ocean Energy		Technologies related to ocean energy are being developed to exploit the potential of tides and waves and differences in temperature and salinity. The development of this emerging industry will not only contribute to achieving our goals of renewable energies and reducing greenhouse gas emissions, but also to stimulate economic growth through innovation and create new high-quality jobs.
	Mining of the seabed		In the EU there are currently many organizations engaged in mineral extraction activities, both as technology providers and as mining operators. The European Commission has undertaken several studies and projects aimed at shedding light on the benefits, drawbacks and gaps in knowledge related to this type of extractions
	Coastal Tourism		The coastal and maritime tourism industry is part of the "blue growth" strategy of the EU and has been defined as an area with special potential to promote an intelligent, sustainable and inclusive Europe

Source: adapted fromEuropean Commission (2012)

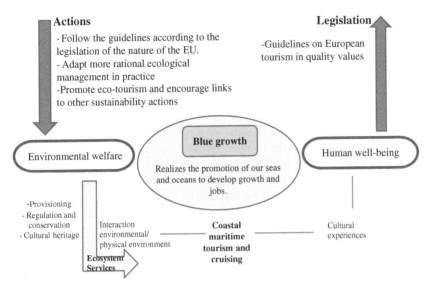

Figure 1. Balance between blue growth and tourism.
Source: Adapted from Lillebø et al. (2017).

The concept of blue tourism, which can be understood as that tourism carried out on the coast or at sea, is capable of incorporating, to the quality of the service offered, the three facets of sustainability: economic, social and environmental, for minimize negative impacts on the natural ecosystem and the local economy. So we define blue tourism as one that develops in coastal and maritime areas in line with the principles of Blue Growth for the preservation of the natural environment, respecting the marine habitats sources of wealth and the *raison d'être* of such tourism. Therefore, blue tourism must first and foremost be a sustainable tourism, to then become a natural conservation agent and a driver of competitive advantages for companies that bet on it. Thus, blue growth requires a balance between the social, economic and environmental aspects supported by the services of the marine ecosystem (Lillebø et al., 2017). Figure 1 shows the balance between blue growth and tourism.

Nautical tourism to the three perspectives of Blue Growth

Currently, tourism is one of the largest economic activities in the world with a positive impact on economic growth and employment (Franzoni, 2015). Among all the human activities that take place at sea, one of the most important and that has grown in recent years is the coastal and maritime tourism industry (Papageorgiou, 2016). This tourist industry is known as nautical tourism. Hence, nautical tourism includes different types of activities related to the sea or water. Nautical tourism can be classified into two types: (1) coastal tourism and (2) maritime tourism.

Coastal tourism is tourism in which water is the predominant element, mainly sun and beach tourism and related activities, such as swimming, sunbathing, coastal routes (coastal trekking, tourism cycle, etc.). This sun and beach tourism attracts three of every four tourists in Spain (Alves, Ballester, Rigall-I-Torrent, Ferreira, & Benavente, 2017) and something similar is going on at Portugal (Almeida, Costa, & Nunes da Silva, 2017).

Maritime tourism is one that its activities develop properly in the seas and oceans. The most outstanding activity is the cruises (Papageorgiou, 2016) but also include activities such as water sports (sailing, scuba diving, underwater fishing, sport fishing, wind surfing, surfing, water skiing), tours to marine parks for the observation of wild life and observation of marine mammals (dolphins, whales, etc.).

Nowadays, nautical tourism has become the largest maritime economic activity, employing 2.35 million people (1.1% of total employment in the EU) (European Commission, 2012). However, the concentration of tourists in a geographical area can lead to risk of damage and the irregular consumption of natural resources (Almeida et al., 2017) and much of the value of coastal and marine environments are outside the market (Alves et al., 2017).

Maritime and coastal tourism also faces sustainability challenges. Many coastal areas are fragile, and recent decades have shown that tourism activities and, in particular, mass tourism can endanger local ecosystems, as well as the general attractiveness of these areas (García-Ayllón, 2015).

Sustainability is a condition for the competitiveness of a tourist destination. This competitiveness can be defined as "the capacity of the destination to create and integrate value-added products to help maintain market position or even improve it in the long term" (d'Hauteserre, 2000). Moreover, sustainability is based on the idea of meeting the needs of the present without compromising the ability of future generations to meet their own needs and has been progressively introduced into the strategic management of organizations taking into account factors such as the preservation of the environment, well-being human rights or human rights and social cohesion (Moneva & Ortas, 2010).

Methodology

The methodology used for this work is based on the Delphi method. Linstone and Turoff (1975) defined the Delphi technique as a *"method of structuring a group communication process that is effective in allowing a group of individuals, as a whole, to deal with a complex problem."* This prospective method seeks to approach the consensus of a group of experts based on the analysis and reflection of a defined problem (Varela-Ruiz, Díaz-Bravo, & García-Durán, 2012). This technique is chosen because it has been previously used in similar investigations (Blasco Mira, López Padrón, & Mengual Andrés, 2010). The Delphi method is an effective procedure (Linstone & Turoff, 1975) and systematic procedure that aims to gather expert opinions on a particular topic in order to incorporate these judgments into the configuration of a questionnaire and achieve consensus through the convergence of expert opinions geographically disseminated (Blasco Mira et al., 2010).

This technique aims to be a systematic and interactive method aimed at gathering the opinions of a group of experts (Seguí-Mas & Server, 2010) and can be used for two fundamental purposes (Dalkey & Helmer, 1963): (1) predictive purposes: the method as a forecasting technique in conditions of uncertainty about future scenarios and it is the best-known utility; (2) obtaining opinion on a specific topic for which prior information is not available.

The use of the Delphi Method as a validation tool for questionnaires has been widely used in numerous studies and fields of knowledge (Hung, Altschuld, & Lee, 2008). So, we use this technique in this work for the validation of a questionnaire on blue growth and tourism since what is pursued with this technique is to obtain the degree of consensus or agreement of the specialists on the problem raised instead of leave the decision to a single professional. Three of its basic premises stand out (Varela-Ruiz et al., 2012): (1) in non-exact disciplines, *in situ*ations of uncertainty or when objective information is lacking, it is appropriate to use the subjective judgment of experts as a resource; (2) the subjective judgment of a single expert is subject to numerous biases and imperfections, and being limited to a person's knowledge and experience usually results in an imprecise estimate; (3) the quality of subjective group judgment is generally superior to that of an individual due to the greater information available to a group.

Ortega-Mohedano (2008) poses a series of steps to follow for the correct application of the Delphi method. The phases of which the method consists are the following: (1) definition of the problem; (2) formation of a group that addresses a specific topic; (3) design of the questionnaire to be used; (4) delivery of the questionnaire to the panel of experts; (5) analysis of the answers to the questionnaire; (6) preparation, delivery and analysis of successive rounds if necessary; and (7) report of analysis of results and conclusions of the work.

In this study we will use a version of the method called "modified Delphi" (Varela-Ruiz et al., 2012). Unlike the original version of the method, in which three or more rounds of consultations are carried out, two rounds are performed in the modified Delphi. The reasons for using this version are the following: (1) a Delphi study with many phases is a long and expensive process for both the researcher and the experts; (2) each additional round reduces the number of responses, limiting the effectiveness of the study; and (3) with two rounds it is easy to keep the attention of the experts.

Formation of a group that addresses a specific topic

Two working groups in charge of validating the designed questionnaire were formed, in this case the coordinating team and the panel of experts. According to Landeta (1999) the minimum number of experts for an investigation using the Delphi method must be between 7 and 50. The coordinating team is formed by a member of the Department of Business Economics of the Technical University of Cartagena (UPCT), a member of the Department of Economic and Juridical Sciences of the University Centre of the Defence (CUD), both Ph.D.

The selection of the group of experts was made by the coordinating team, for which the first step was to establish as a fundamental criterion of selection and competence of the candidates in the area of knowledge, since they are either academic researchers related to the topic to be studied or professionals in the tourism industry. Table 2 shows in a more detailed way the members that make up the group of experts.

Design of the questionnaire to be used

A questionnaire has been prepared following the existing literature on blue growth, analyzed in Section 2, focusing on tourism. For the construction of the Delphi questionnaire, a Likert scale of 5 points has been used, where 1 corresponds to "nothing in agreement" and 5 to "very or totally agree", with an intermediate point 3 that reflects indifference with the item analyzed, as it is a scale used in similar studies (e.g. Blasco Mira et al., 2010).Thus, the questionnaire was made as follows: The first six questions refer to what is known as sociodemographic data (type of activity, seniority, type of company, etc.).Question 7 refers to the implementation of some type of standardized management systems of both quality and environment; question 8 refers to the conditions or motivations for nautical tourism; question 9 deals with the influence of nautical tourism on infrastructures and facilities; question 10, deals with the social impact; question 11 deals with environmental impact and sustainability; question 12 refers to the economic impact of tourism activities and finally question 13 is an open question for any question that the respondent wants to point out.

Table 2. Group of experts.

Institution	Education	Position	Experience
UPCT	Doctor (PhD)	Professor and researcher	18 years
Universidad de Cantabria	Doctor (PhD)	Professor and researcher	≥ 5 years
Instituto Politecnico Setúbal	Doctor (PhD)	Professor and researcher	> 20 years
UPCT	Master (MSc)	Student/professional	5/1 years
UPCT	Master (MSc)	Student/professional	5/1 years
UPCT	Master (MSc)	Student/professional	5/1 years
Hotel	Master (MSc)	Staff	> 1 years
Diving club	Graduate	Manager	> 5 years
Sailing School	High school	Manager	> 15 years
Marina	Bachelor	Manager	> 5 years
Marina	Bachelor	Manager	> 10 years
Hotel	Graduate	Manager	> 15 years

Delivery of the questionnaire to the panel of experts

The panel of experts in this phase consisted of 12 people who were divided into three groups (teaching staff, master students and professionals of the industry) to make a prior assessment of the questionnaire. It is considered that the number of experts is methodologically reliable following (Ortega-Mohedano, 2008). Each group assessed the items and marked those items that according to their criteria were important and more clear when assessing the relationship between tourism and blue growth. The questionnaire was delivered at the final four-month 2017.

Analysis of the answers to the questionnaire

Once the answers have been received, an analysis of them is made taking into account the average of the values obtained for each item and its standard deviation (SD). It is considered that there is no consensus among experts when the average score obtained for a given item is less than 3 points. On the one hand, the analysis is performed globally for the total of the 12 responses received, identifying which of the items do not generate consensus among the experts. On the other hand, anonymity is guaranteed among the experts consulted, who have not had contact with each other to complete the questionnaire. All the items get an average higher than 3, so all of them are accepted. Although some of them have a high standard deviation, which denotes disparity of scores among the experts.

Preparation, delivery and analysis of successive rounds

In the previous phase, some experts suggested including the following two items as a question-naire item in reference to nautical tourism and with respect to infrastructures: (1) the develop-ment of infrastructures should consider the preservation of areas for biodiversity and natural conservation and (2) the offer of other complementary activities such as, for example, the creation of bars and restaurants. Another expert suggested defining sustainable areas for tourism activities (with nature conservation) and promoting such activities involving the local community. Finally, another expert suggested that nautical tourism can be favoured by the existence of an adequate cultural and historical offer. So in this third phase, the questionnaire incorporated such sugges-tions and the modified questionnaire was sent in January 2018.

Results

The results finally obtained are shown in Table 3. In addition, for each dimension studied, the obtained reliability coefficients (Cronbach´s α) are adequate for the nature of this investigation, since they range between 0.789 and 0.959.

In reference to the conditions that promote nautical tourism, experts agree that the most remarkable item is the existence of natural resources followed by climate, with a moderate standard deviation, which shows that the consensus is broad. In reference to tourism have a positive influence on facilities, the experts agree that the most important factor for this is the collaboration between different public institutions, followed by collaboration with private institu-tions. From a social dimension, the experts highlight that nautical tourism improves the external image of the city where it takes place, and it influences positively in the sustainable development what links directly to the Blue Growth.

From an economic point of view, the best-estimated item is that nautical tourism generates employment, followed by access to new markets and that local trade is favoured.

Finally, from the environmental perspective, the experts show a high consensus that nautical tourism promotes the conservation of the maritime or coastal area where it is developed.

Table 3. Results.

Dimensions	Cronbach's α	Items	Average	SD
Conditions for nautical tourism	0.789	An adequate climate is available	4.25	0.754
		There are adequate natural resources	4.17	0.687
		Tourism is seasonal	3.92	1.256
		There are sun and beach	3.92	0.954
		There is an adequate cultural and historical offer	3.83	1.067
		Adequate infrastructures are available	3.75	1.010
Infrastructures	0.891	Creation of Marinas	4.50	0.76
		Creation of Cruise Ports	4.50	0.50
		Expansion of existing infrastructures (e.g. cruise port)	4.58	0.76
		Improves the urban development of the area	4.08	0.86
		Collaboration between institutions (e.g. city council and companies)	4.67	0.75
		Collaboration between different public institutions (e.g. local government and region government)	4.67	0.75
		The offer of other types of complementary activities is improved (restaurants, etc.)	3.75	1.01
		Increase or improve infrastructures for the preservation of areas for biodiversity and natural conservation	3.83	1.07
Social impact	0.900	I consider that nautical tourism favours the management of the cities/municipalities where it is developed	4.25	0.83
		I consider that nautical tourism favours the local community	3.83	0.90
		I consider that nautical tourism favours the development of residents	3.75	1.01
		Tourist activities are developed with respect to the culture of the local community	4.17	0.69
		I consider that nautical tourism favours the education and professional training of residents	3.75	0.83
		The local community recognizes the benefits of this type of tourism	3.67	0.85
		The local community is involved with nautical tourism activities	3.75	0.92
		The local community is concerned about the state of maritime and coastal environments	3.33	1.25
		The nautical tourism favours the sustainable development	3.92	1.11
		The external image of the city is improved	4.00	1.15
		The internal image of the city is improved	3.75	0.92
		The nautical tourism favours the sponsorship of cultural and sports actions of the community	3.83	0.90
Economic Impact	0.959	I consider that nautical tourism generates employment	4.50	0.76
		I think that nautical tourism increases stable employment	4.08	0.95
		I consider that nautical tourism increases the prices, e.g. of food and drinks. housing rentals, etc.	3.67	0.75
		I think that nautical tourism favours local businesses and businesses	4.33	0.75
		I think that nautical tourism favours the businesses and franchisees of large companies	4.33	0.75
		Tourism implies an increase in investments in infrastructure	4.33	0.94
		Through tourism there is access to new markets or customers	4.33	0.85
		The nautical tourism offers competitive advantages with respect to another kind of tourism	3.83	0.69
		Collaborations with other tourism organizations are obtained	3.83	0.80
		This kind of tourism industry favours the continuous training of workers	3.67	0.94
Environmental Impact	0.914	I think that nautical tourism improves waste management directly or indirectly	3.67	0.75
		I consider that nautical tourism encourages the conservation of this maritime or coastal area	4.33	0.75
		I consider that nautical tourism increases the degree of environmental education in the area	4.17	0.99
		The activities of the nautical tourism are respectful with the Environment	4.17	0.80
		The tourist appreciates the conservation of natural spaces	4.25	0.72
		Increase environmental training of employees	3.75	0.83
		Nautical tourism favours the sustainable development	3.92	0.86
		Nautical tourism allows the definition of sustainable areas	3.67	0.75

In general terms, all the items have been accepted by the experts, some with a large consensus measured through the low or moderate standard deviation. Those who show a high standard deviation above 1 have been accepted but knowing that there is disparity in their scores.

Conclusion and implications

As a main conclusion of the work carried out, a questionnaire has been validated and a series of future research lines have been obtained in relation to the strategies and policies on Blue Growth and Blue Tourism.

A group of experts has been consulted about the variables that measure blue tourism and a questionnaire has been formulated to contrast empirically through field work, in a future investigation, the theoretical blue growth model proposed. The final questionnaire has been enriched with the contributions and suggestions of the experts. The indicators extracted from the experts' assessment are in line with other similar studies (e.g. Lucrezi et al., 2017), emphasizing that the existence of natural resources and climatic conditions are fundamental for nautical tourism, as well as collaboration between public and private institutions. On the other hand, the importance of such tourism can enhance the image of the city as a tourist destination and is generating new jobs and can further promote local commerce, previously established. Finally, nautical tourism can promote the conservation of maritime or coastal areas, thus favouring sustainable development and positively influencing sustainability.

Taking into account the very magnitude of the industry and its strong impact in many European coastal and marine areas, as well as the precariousness and scarce qualification of a large part of its current labour (European Commission, 2012), nautical tourism can contribute to the general development of the economy of the area where they carry out their activities and can contribute to the creation of jobs for residents and be qualified jobs, so the tourism training is a factor to take into account for the quality of the service offered, as revealed by the data obtained through the Delphi method developed here. The experts valuate very well those issues related to education and training, as well as those that refer to the generation of employment and local development. However, in the questions about the involvement of the local community or the perception of this about nautical tourism it seems that this community is insufficiently involved with tourism so it is necessary to investigate more in this regard.

The efforts of this blue tourism that we propose should reach and ensure a good environmental protection of the coast and marine spaces, tourism activities should mitigate environmental degradation and finally tourism activities and their associated infrastructures should be adapted to the needs of the local community.

Hence, this work tries to be a starting point to establish the relationships between tourism and ecology that should be taken into account when developing tourism business models while relating the capacity of coastal destinations with the blue growth. In this sense, given that nautical tourism can be practiced at any time, it may be important to analyze seasonality within the tourist offer. Undoubtedly, followed by this line of research, natural resources, the quality of the waters and the beauty of the landscape are important factors to attract this type of tourism.

The present study presents a series of limitations that should be noted and taken into account for an improvement of the research. The first limitation has to do with the technique used, since it has been difficult to find collaboration to form the group of experts. A second limitation has to do with the statistical treatment carried out, because the lack of adequate statistical information means that the study must be expanded with field work and a larger sample where nautical tourist businesses are asked to respond to the survey in order to process the data with a quantitative technique, which allows to establish future lines of work and research.

Disclosure statement

No potential conflict of interest was reported by the authors.

ORCID

Juan Andrés Bernal Conesa (iD) http://orcid.org/0000-0003-4626-4805
Antonio Juan Briones Peñalver (iD) http://orcid.org/0000-0002-2893-007X

References

Almeida, J., Costa, C., & Nunes da Silva, F. (2017). A framework for conflict analysis in spatial planning for tourism. *Tourism Management Perspectives, 24*, 94–106.

Alves, B., Ballester, R., Rigall-I-Torrent, R., Ferreira, Ó., & Benavente, J. (2017). How feasible is coastal management? A social benefit analysis of a coastal destination in SW Spain. *Tourism Management, 60*, 188–200.

Anonymous. (2016, September 28). Crecimiento azul [Blue Growth]. Retrieved October 7, 2017, from https://ec.europa.eu/maritimeaffairs/policy/blue_growth_es

Blasco Mira, J. E., López Padrón, A., & Mengual Andrés, S. (2010). Validación mediante el método Delphi de un cuestionario para conocer las experiencias e interés hacia las actividades acuáticas con especial atención al Winsurf [Delphi Method validation of a questionnaire to get experience and interest in Water activities with special attention to windsurfing]. *Agora Para La Educación Física Y El Deporte, 12*(1), 75–96. Retrieved from http://roderic.uv.es/handle/10550/51736

Burgess, M. G., Clemence, M., McDermott, G. R., Costello, C., & Gaines, S. D. (2016). Five rules for pragmatic blue growth. *Marine Policy, 87*, 331–339.

d'Hauteserre, A. M. (2000). Lessons in managed destination competitiveness: The case of Foxwoods casino resort. *Tourism Management, 21*(1), 23–32.

Dalkey, N., & Helmer, O. (1963). An experimental application of the delphi method to the use of experts. *Management Science, 9*(3), 458–467.

European Commission. (2012). *Communication from the Commission to the European Parliament, the Council, the European Economic and Social Committee and the Committee of the Regions*. Brussels: Blue growth. Opportunities for marine and maritime sustainable growth.

Franzoni, S. (2015). Measuring the sustainability performance of the tourism sector. *Tourism Management Perspectives, 16*, 22–27.

Frazao Santos, C., Domingos, T., Ferreira, M. A., Orbach, M., & Andrade, F. (2014). How sustainable is sustainable marine spatial planning? Part II? The Portuguese experience. *Marine Policy, 49*, 48–58.

García-Ayllón, S. (2015). La Manga case study: Consequences from short-term urban planning in a tourism mass destiny of the Spanish Mediterranean coast. *Cities, 43*, 141–151.

Hung, H.-L., Altschuld, J. W., & Lee, Y.-F. (2008). Methodological and conceptual issues confronting a cross-country Delphi study of educational program evaluation. *Evaluation and Program Planning, 31*(2), 191–198.

Landeta, J. (1999). *El método Delphi, una técnica de previsión del futuro* [The Delphi Method, a forecasting technique for the future]. Barcelona: Ariel S.A.

Lillebø, A. I., Pita, C., Garcia Rodrigues, J., Ramos, S., & Villasante, S. (2017). How can marine ecosystem services support the Blue Growth agenda? *Marine Policy, 81*, 132–142.

Linstone, H. A., & Turoff, M. (1975). *The Delphi method: Techniques and applications.* California: Addison-Wesley Pub. Co., Advanced Book Program.

Lucrezi, S., Milanese, M., Markantonatou, V., Cerrano, C., Sarà, A., Palma, M., & Saayman, M. (2017). Scuba diving tourism systems and sustainability: Perceptions by the scuba diving industry in two Marine Protected Areas. *Tourism Management, 59*, 385–403.

Moneva, J. M., & Ortas, E. (2010). Corporate environmental and financial performance: A multivariate approach. *Industrial Management & Data Systems, 110*(2), 193–210.

Mulazzani, L., Trevisi, R., Manrique, R., & Malorgio, G. (2016). Blue Growth and the relationship between ecosystem services and human activities: The Salento artisanal fisheries case study. *Ocean & Coastal Management, 134*, 120–128.

Ortega-Mohedano, F. (2008). El método Delphi, prospectiva en Ciencias Sociales a través del análisis de un caso práctico [The Delphi method, prospective in social sciences through the analysis of a practical case]. *Revista EAN, 64*, 31–54.

Papageorgiou, M. (2016). Coastal and marine tourism: A challenging factor in Marine Spatial Planning. *Ocean & Coastal Management, 129*, 44–48.

Pauli, G. (2015). *La economía azul* [The Blue Economy]. Barcelona: Tusquets Editores.

Pinto, H., Cruz, A. R., & Combe, C. (2015). Cooperation and the emergence of maritime clusters in the Atlantic: Analysis and implications of innovation and human capital for blue growth. *Marine Policy, 57*, 167–177.

Rodríguez-Rodríguez, D., Malak, D. A., Soukissian, T., & Sánchez-Espinosa, A. (2016). Achieving Blue Growth through maritime spatial planning: Offshore wind energy optimization and biodiversity conservation in Spain. *Marine Policy, 73*, 8–14.

Seguí-Mas, E., & Server, R. (2010). Caracterización del business capital de las cooperativas de crédito a través del análisis Delphi [Characterization of the business capital of credit cooperatives through the Delphi analysis]. *REVESCO: Revista De Estudios Cooperativos, 103*(3), 101–122.

Varela-Ruiz, M., Díaz-Bravo, L., & García-Durán, R. (2012). Descripción y usos del método Delphi en investigaciones del área de la salud [Description and uses of the Delphi method in health sciences research]. *Investigación En Educación Médica, 1*(2), 90–95.

Index

Page numbers in **bold** refer to tables and those in *italic* refer to figures.

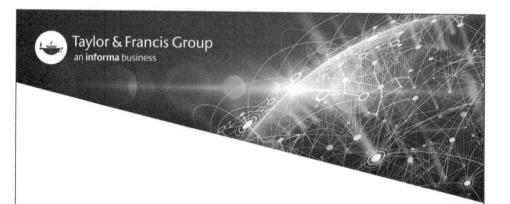

For Product Safety Concerns and Information please contact our
EU representative GPSR@taylorandfrancis.com Taylor & Francis
Verlag GmbH, Kaufingerstraße 24, 80331 München, Germany